Descendants of George R. Casto

Generation 1

1. **GEORGE R.**[1] **CASTO** was born on 26 Jul 1826 in Virginia. He died on 04 Mar 1903 in Parchment Valley, Jackson County, West Virginia. He married (1) **SUSANNA DEWEES**, daughter of Samuel Dewees and Edith Battin on 12 Apr 1845 in Jackson County, Virginia. She was born on 20 Oct 1823 in Virginia. She died on 10 Sep 1859 in Jackson County, Virginia. He married (2) **WINIFRED (WINNIE) WOODARD**, daughter of John Woodard and Mary Martin on 07 Nov 1861 in Parchment Valley, Jackson County, Virginia. She was born in Jan 1838 in Meigs County, Ohio. She died in 1910 in Ripley, Jackson County, West Virginia.

More About George R. Casto:
Burial: Pleasant Hill Cemetery, Parchment Valley, Jackson County, West Virginia Cause Of Death: Dropsy
Living In: 1860 George and his children, Samuel, George, Margaret and Edmond are living with his brother William, and his family in Jackson County, Virginia.
Occupation: 1850 in District 27, Jackson County, Virginia; Farmer
Occupation: 1860 in Jackson County, Virginia; Farm Labor
Occupation: 1870 in Union Township, Jackson County, West Virginia; Farmer
Occupation: 1880 in Union District, Jackson County, West Virginia; Laborer
Occupation: 1900 in Ripley District, Jackson County, West Virginia; Farmer

More About Susanna Dewees:
Burial: Pleasant Hill Cemetery, Given, Jackson County, West Virginia
Cause Of Death: Confinement

Notes for Susanna Dewees:
Marriage record has first name as Susan.

Date of death on death record is September 10, 1859. Headstone has April 10, 1857 for date of death. Death record for John Casto has 1859 for year of death and John being six months old.

More About George R. Casto and Susanna
Dewees: Marriage Fact: Married by E. J. Rollins

George R. Casto and Susanna Dewees had the following children:

2.   i. SAMUEL DANIEL[2] CASTO was born on 05 Apr 1846 in Jackson County, Virginia. He died on 16 Mar 1923 in Ripley, Jackson County, West Virginia. He married (1) MARY EMILY FLOWERS, daughter of Thomas Flowers and Emily Jane Sayre on 29 Dec 1877 in Jackson County, West Virginia. She was born in Sep 1852 in Virginia. She died before 16 Mar 1923. He married (2) AMANDA JANE ANKRUM, daughter of William C. Ankrum and Ruth (unknown) on 11 Dec 1871 in Jackson County, West Virginia. She was born on 22 Feb 1837 in Jackson County, Virginia. She died on 08 May 1877 in Jackson County, West Virginia.

3.   ii. GEORGE WASHINGTON CASTO was born on 09 Aug 1847 in Jackson County, Virginia. He died on 13 Nov 1926 in Falls Township, Hocking County, Ohio. He married (1) MARGARET FRANCES JOHNSTON, daughter of Abraham E. Johnston and Susan L. McMillan on 14 Dec 1878 in Mason County, West Virginia. She was born on 08 Dec 1856 in Grafton, Taylor County, Virginia. She died on 29 Dec 1928 in Marion Township, Franklin County, Ohio. He married (2) CASSANDRA CATHERINE BARBER, daughter of Sal Barber and C. (unknown) on 20 Sep 1870 in Jackson County, West Virginia. She was born about 1855 in Ohio. She died about 1877.

iii. MARTHA JANE CASTO was born on 16 Dec 1849 in Jackson County, Virginia. She died on 22 Feb 1933 in Millwood, Jackson County, West Virginia. She married Richard Ankrum, son of William C. Ankrum and Ruth (unknown) on 12 Mar 1868 in Jackson County, West Virginia. He was born in Oct 1834 in Tyler County, Virginia. He died on 21 Nov 1909 in Millwood, Jackson County, West Virginia.

More About Martha Jane Casto:
Burial: 24 Feb 1933 in Ankrum Cemetery
Living In: 1860 With Alfred Dewees and his family in Jackson County, Virginia

iv. LYDIA CASTO was born in Jun 1850 in Jackson County, Virginia.

v. MARGARET CASTO was born about 1853 in Jackson County, Virginia.

vi. EDMOND R. CASTO was born in Jan 1857 in Jackson County, Virginia. He died in Mar 1877 in Mason County, West Virginia.

vii. JOHN CASTO was born in 1859 in Jackson County, Virginia. He died in 1859 in Jackson County, Virginia.

More About John Casto:
Cause Of Death: Bowel Complications

Notes for John Casto:
Lived for six months.

More About Winifred (Winnie)
Woodard: Cause Of Death: Dropsy
Living In: 1860 With Lewis Curtis and his wife in Ripley, Jackson County, West Virginia
Living In: 1910 With her son, Charles, and his family in Ripley District, Jackson County, West Virginia.

Notes for Winifred (Winnie) Woodard:
Marriage license issued on November 5, 1861 in Jackson County, Virginia.

Death was in 1910, after April 26.

George R. Casto and Winifred (Winnie) Woodard had the following children:

viii. MARTIN A. CASTO was born on 25 May 1862 in Jackson County, Virginia.

ix. LEWIS ALLEN CASTO was born on 03 Feb 1864 in Jackson County, West Virginia. He died on 12 Mar 1945 in Logan, Hocking County, Ohio.

More About Lewis Allen Casto:
Burial: 15 Mar 1945 in Oak Grove Cemetery, Logan, Hocking County, Ohio

x. ANGELINA ELECTA CASTO was born on 10 Mar 1866 in Ripley, Jackson County, West Virginia. She died on 17 Jun 1936 in Crooksville, Perry County, Ohio. She married GEORGE A. RUSSELL.

More About Angelina Electa Casto:
Burial: 19 Jun 1936 in Crooksville, Perry County, Ohio

xi.   MARY CORDELIA CASTO was born on 10 Mar 1868 in Jackson County, West Virginia.
She died on 05 Feb 1929 in Fremont, Sandusky County, Ohio. She married Charles
Applegate, son of James R. Applegate and Sarah Ogden on 01 Nov 1913 in Hocking
County, Ohio. He was born on 30 Jun 1868 in Hocking County, Ohio.

More About Mary Cordelia Casto:
Burial: 08 Feb 1929 in Logan, Ohio

xii.   ELIZA CASTO was born about 1870 in West Virginia.

xiii.   CHARLES WILBER CASTO was born on 22 Feb 1875 in Jackson County, West
Virginia. He died on 06 Dec 1951 in Logan, Hocking County, Ohio. He
married Rettie Board on 11 Sep 1904 in Jackson County, West Virginia. She
was born about 1877 in Jackson County, West Virginia.

More About Charles Wilber Casto:
Burial: 08 Dec 1951 in Smith Chapel Cemetery, Logan, Hocking County, Ohio
Occupation: 1910 in Ripley District, Jackson County, West Virginia; Farmer

xiv.   HANNAH E. CASTO was born in Feb 1883 in Jackson County, West Virginia.

Generation 2

2.   SAMUEL DANIEL² CASTO (George R.¹) was born on 05 Apr 1846 in Jackson County, Virginia. He
died on 16 Mar 1923 in Ripley, Jackson County, West Virginia. He married (1) MARY EMILY
FLOWERS, daughter of Thomas Flowers and Emily Jane Sayre on 29 Dec 1877 in Jackson
County, West Virginia. She was born in Sep 1852 in Virginia. She died before 16 Mar 1923. He
married (2) AMANDA JANE ANKRUM, daughter of William C. Ankrum and Ruth (unknown) on 11
Dec 1871 in Jackson County, West Virginia. She was born on 22 Feb 1837 in Jackson County,
Virginia. She died on 08 May 1877 in Jackson County, West Virginia.

More About Samuel Daniel Casto:
Burial: 19 Mar 1923 in United Methodist Church Cemetery, Cottageville, Jackson County,
West Virginia
Cause Of Death: Pneumonia
Living In: 1870 With William C. Ankrum and his family in Jackson County, West Virginia.
Occupation: Farmer

Notes for Mary Emily Flowers:
Marriage license issued on December 29, 1877.

Samuel Daniel Casto and Mary Emily Flowers had the following children:

i.   GEORGE M.³ CASTO was born in Oct 1881 in West Virginia.

ii.   SAMUEL E. CASTO was born in Sep 1887 in West Virginia.

iii.   CYNTHIA A. CASTO was born in Jun 1894 in West Virginia.

More About Amanda Jane Ankrum:
Burial: United Methodist Church Cemetery, Cottageville, Jackson County, West Virginia

Notes for Amanda Jane Ankrum:
Headstone gives her age as 40 years, 2 months and 14 days on May 8, 1877.

3.   **GEORGE WASHINGTON**[2] **CASTO** (George R.[1]) was born on 09 Aug 1847 in Jackson County, Virginia. He died on 13 Nov 1926 in Falls Township, Hocking County, Ohio. He married (1) **MARGARET FRANCES JOHNSTON**, daughter of Abraham E. Johnston and Susan L. McMillan on 14 Dec 1878 in Mason County, West Virginia. She was born on 08 Dec 1856 in Grafton, Taylor County, Virginia. She died on 29 Dec 1928 in Marion Township, Franklin County, Ohio. He married (2) **CASSANDRA CATHERINE BARBER**, daughter of Sal Barber and C. (unknown) on 20 Sep 1870 in Jackson County, West Virginia. She was born about 1855 in Ohio. She died about 1877.

More About George Washington Casto:
Burial: 15 Nov 1926 in Oak Grove Cemetery, Logan, Hocking County, Ohio
Living In: 1870 With his father and step mother in Union Township, Jackson County, West Virginia.
Occupation: 1870 in Union Township, Jackson County, West Virginia; Farm Laborer
Occupation: 1880 in Cologne District, Mason County, West Virginia; Farm Laborer
Occupation: 1900 in Ripley District, Jackson County, West Virginia; Farmer
Occupation: 1910 in Logan, Hocking County, Ohio; Odd Jobs Laborer
Occupation: 1920 in Falls Township, Hocking County, Ohio; General Farm Laborer

More About Margaret Frances Johnston:
Burial: 31 Dec 1928 in Oak Grove Cemetery, Logan, Hocking County,
Ohio Cause Of Death: Organic Heart Trouble
Occupation: 1910 in Logan, Hocking County, Ohio; At Home Washerwoman

More About George Washington Casto and Margaret Frances Johnston: Marriage
Fact: Married in the home of the Bride's father by B.A. Armstrong, M.G.

George Washington Casto and Margaret Frances Johnston had the following children:

4.   i. CORA BELLE[3] CASTO was born on 02 Nov 1879 in Mason County, West Virginia. She died on 27 Apr 1956 in Jackson County, West Virginia. She married George Wilman Lathey, son of Joseph W. Lathey and Emma Ward on 26 Feb 1899 in Center Point School House, Jackson County, West Virginia. He was born on 07 May 1878 in Meigs County, Ohio. He died on 16 Dec 1945 in Friendly, Pleasants County, West Virginia.

         ii. ROSA ELLEN CASTO was born on 28 Aug 1881 in Cottageville, Jackson County, West Virginia. She died on 29 Jan 1976 in Mansfield, Richland County, Ohio. She married (1) KELLEY FREEMAN KAY, son of John Kay and Catherine (unknown) on 20 Jan 1901 in Jackson County, West Virginia. He was born on 22 Dec 1877 in Jackson County, West Virginia. He died on 30 Oct 1918 in Logan, Hocking County, Ohio. She married (2) FRANK ELMER WOLFE, son of David Wolfe and Mary Mowery on 20 Feb 1926 in Franklin County, ohio. He was born on 19 May 1884 in Hocking county, Ohio. He died on 11 Jun 1950 in Cleveland, Cuyahoga County, Ohio. She married (3) ALBERT BURKHART, son of Fred Burkhart and Mary Haggi on 21 Apr 1939 in Perry County, Ohio. He was born on 30 Jan 1896 in Ohio. He died on 16 Dec 1968 in Columbus, Franklin County, Ohio.

         More About Rosa Ellen Casto:

Burial: Oak Grove Cemetery, Logan, Hocking County, Ohio
Living In: 1976 Last residence was in Logan, Hocking County, Ohio

5.　　　iii. MIRANDA NICHOLAS CASTO was born on 09 Aug 1883 in Cottageville, Jackson County, West Virginia. He died on 27 Jan 1971 in Hocking County, Ohio. He married (1) BESSIE LOUESA RUBLE, daughter of James Merley Ruble and Mary Jane Poling on 29 Jan 1907 in Hocking County, Ohio. She was born on 03 Jan 1883 in Falls Township, Hocking County, Ohio. She died in 1955. He married (2) XEMA BRAY VEST, daughter of Joseph Vest and Clara M. Bray on 07 Jun 1958 in Hocking County, Ohio. She was born on 26 Mar 1889 in Benton Township, Hocking County, Ohio. She died on 10 Apr 1987 in Logan, Hocking County, Ohio.

6.　　　iv. SUSAN ELPHA CASTO was born on 27 May 1886 in Jackson County, West Virginia. She married (1) JAMES DARLINGTON COAKLEY, son of Augustus Coakley and Margaret Joy on 29 May 1903 in Hocking County, Ohio. He was born on 27 Dec 1877 in York Township, Athens County, Ohio. He died on 01 Feb 1954 in Lancaster, Ohio. She married (2) JOSEPH EDGAR LATTIMER, son of David Lattimer and Catherine Willison on 30 Dec 1919 in Hocking County, Ohio. He was born on 24 Aug 1890 in Starr Township, Hocking County, Ohio. He died on 07 Mar 1971 in Hocking County, Ohio.

　　　　v. A. J. CASTO was born on 06 Oct 1888 in Jackson County, West Virginia. She died before 16 Jun 1900.

Notes for A. J. Casto:
Birth date and gender are from birth record.

7.　　　vi. ROBERT EDWARD CASTO was born on 03 Mar 1891 in Cologne District, Mason County, West Virginia. He died on 13 Oct 1958 in Columbus, Franklin County, Ohio. He married MARY E. FRIEND. She was born on 17 Feb 1896 in Groveport, Franklin County, Ohio. She died on 13 Nov 1978 in Columbus, Franklin County, Ohio.

8.　　　vii. ELSIE MYRTLE CASTO was born on 15 Jun 1893 in Jackson County, West Virginia. She died on 09 Nov 1957 in Ohio. She married Van Robert Stewart, son of Henry W. Stewart and Deborah McDaniel on 28 May 1910 in Gallia County, Ohio. He was born on 01 Sep 1863 in Mason County, West Virginia. He died on 07 Nov 1939 in Falls Township, Hocking County, Ohio.

　　　　viii. LESTIE GERTRUDE CASTO was born on 08 Aug 1896 in Jackson County, West Virginia. She married (1) JAMES EVERETT STEWART, son of Van Robert Stewart and Cora B. Swan on 14 Jun 1913 in Hocking County, Ohio. He was born on 25 Jan 1891 in Silex, Lincoln County, Missouri. He died in Oct 1963 in West Virginia. She married (2) ABRAM BARBER, son of Jared Barber and Alice H. Walls on 04 Aug 1923 in Franklin County, Ohio. He was born on 14 Jul 1895 in Mundy, Hocking County, Ohio. He died on 25 Jul 1964 in Nelsonville, Athens County, Ohio.

More About Lestie Gertrude Casto:
Living In: 1913 Logan, Hocking County, Ohio
Living In: 27 Jan 1920 living as Gertrude Casto with Van Robert Stewart and his family in Green Township, Hocking County, Ohio.
Living In: 1923 Franklin County, Ohio
Occupation: 14 Jun 1913 in Logan, Hocking County, Ohio; Dining Room Girl
Occupation: 1920 in Green Township, Hocking County, Ohio; Cook in hotel Owned by Van Robert Stewart

Notes for Cassandra Catherine Barber:
Marriage record gives her age as 15 at time of her marriage.

George Washington Casto and Cassandra Catherine Barber had the following children:

    ix.   MAGGIE MAY CASTO was born on 06 Jun 1873 in Olive Township, Meigs County, Ohio. She died on 29 Nov 1946 in Columbus, Franklin County, Ohio. She married (1) GEORGE W. EDMONDS, son of Peter Edmonds and Susan (unknown) on 22 Apr 1891 in Jackson County, West Virginia. He was born on 17 Jul 1854 in Greenbrier County, West Virginia. He died on 28 Sep 1930 in Columbus, Franklin County, Ohio. She married (2) JOHN L. MANLEY, son of John Manley and Elizabeth Lewis on 17 Jul 1917 in Franklin County, Ohio. He was born on 26 Nov 1869 in Cheshire Township, Gallia County, Ohio. He died on 21 Nov 1942 in Columbus, Franklin County, Ohio.

More About Maggie May Casto:
Burial: 02 Dec 1946 in Groveport Cemetery, Groveport, Franklin County, Ohio

Notes for Maggie May Casto:
Headstone indicates she is buried beside her first husband, George Edmonds.
----

    x.   CHARLES CASTO was born about 1875 in West Virginia.

Generation 3

4.   CORA BELLE[3] CASTO (George Washington[2], George R.[1]) was born on 02 Nov 1879 in Mason County, West Virginia. She died on 27 Apr 1956 in Jackson County, West Virginia. She married George Wilman Lathey, son of Joseph W. Lathey and Emma Ward on 26 Feb 1899 in Center Point School House, Jackson County, West Virginia. He was born on 07 May 1878 in Meigs County, Ohio. He died on 16 Dec 1945 in Friendly, Pleasants County, West Virginia.

More About Cora Belle Casto:
Burial: Foster Chapel Cemetery, Evans, Jackson County, West Virginia

More About George Wilman Lathey:
Burial: 18 Dec 1945 in Foster Chapel Cemetery, Evans, Jackson County, West Virginia
Cause Of Death: Myocarditis
Occupation: Farmer

George Wilman Lathey and Cora Belle Casto had the following children:

    i.   VALCIE J.[4] LATHEY was born on 01 Oct 1899 in West Virginia. He died on 24 Oct 1963 in Morgantown, West Virginia.

More About Valcie J. Lathey:
Burial: 26 Oct 1963 in Letart, West Virginia
Cause Of Death: Staphylococcal Pneumonia
Occupation: Minister

    ii.   DELA DORIS LATHEY was born in 1901. She died in 1929.

    iii.   IVA GLADYS LATHEY was born on 12 Sep 1902 in Rockcastle, Jackson County, West

Virginia.

    iv.   ORIS RAY LATHEY was born on 12 Feb 1905 in Rockcastle, Jackson County, West Virginia.

    v.   HARRY C. LATHEY was born in 1908. He died in 1993.

    vi.   CORDA LATHEY was born in 1908.

    vii.   CLYDE LATHEY was born in 1910. He died in 1994.

    viii.   CLARA MARIE LATHEY was born in 1912. She died in 1974.

    ix.   GEORGE WILMAN LATHEY was born in 1914. He died in 1914.

    x.   HOWARD LATHEY was born in 1920. He died in 1983.

5.   **MIRANDA NICHOLAS**[3] **CASTO** (George Washington[2], George R.[1]) was born on 09 Aug 1883 in Cottageville, Jackson County, West Virginia. He died on 27 Jan 1971 in Hocking County, Ohio. He married (1) **BESSIE LOUESA RUBLE**, daughter of James Merley Ruble and Mary Jane Poling on 29 Jan 1907 in Hocking County, Ohio. She was born on 03 Jan 1883 in Falls Township, Hocking County, Ohio. She died in 1955. He married (2) **XEMA BRAY VEST**, daughter of Joseph Vest and Clara M. Bray on 07 Jun 1958 in Hocking County, Ohio. She was born on 26 Mar 1889 in Benton Township, Hocking County, Ohio. She died on 10 Apr 1987 in Logan, Hocking County, Ohio.

More About Miranda Nicholas Casto:
Burial: Oak Grove Cemetery, Logan, Hocking County, Ohio
Living In: 1907   Logan, Ohio
Living In: 1942   Logan, Ohio
Living In: 1971   Logan, Ohio
Occupation: 1942; Working at Hocking Valley Brick Company
Occupation: Minister

Notes for Miranda Nicholas Casto:
World War One and World War Two draft registrations give middle name as Nichola.

More About Bessie Louesa Ruble:
Burial: Oak Grove Cemetery, Logan, Hocking County, Ohio

Notes for Bessie Louesa Ruble:
1900 U.S. census gives name as Lulu Ruble.
Marriage certificate gives name as Lulu Ruble.
Birth record gives name as Bessie Louesa
Ruble. Head Stone gives first name as Louise.
Husband's World War Two draft registration gives Louise as first name of wife.

Miranda Nicholas Casto and Bessie Louesa Ruble had the following children:

    i.   HUBERT FRANKLIN[4] CASTO was born in 1900. He died in 1985.

    ii.   HARRY NICHOLAS CASTO was born in 1907. He died in 1956.

    iii.   ARTHUR EUGENE CASTO was born in 1908. He died in 1975.

    iv.   CLAUDE VERNON CASTO was born in 1911. He died in 1915.

    v.   LAWRENCE EDWARD CASTO was born in 1916. He died in 1992.

    vi.   HAROLD ERNEST CASTO was born in 1921. He died in 1983.

    vii.   ALICE ELANE CASTO was born in 1929. She died in 2003.

More About Xema Bray Vest:
Burial: Fairview Memorial Gardens, Rockbridge, Hocking County, Ohio

Notes for Xema Bray Vest:
Buried beside her first husband, Harley Clinton Kalklosch.

----

6.   **SUSAN ELPHA**^{3} **CASTO** (George Washington^2, George R.^{1}) was born on 27 May 1886 in Jackson County, West Virginia. She married (1) **JAMES DARLINGTON COAKLEY**, son of Augustus Coakley and Margaret Joy on 29 May 1903 in Hocking County, Ohio. He was born on 27 Dec 1877 in York Township, Athens County, Ohio. He died on 01 Feb 1954 in Lancaster, Ohio. She married (2) **JOSEPH EDGAR LATTIMER**, son of David Lattimer and Catherine Willison on 30 Dec 1919 in Hocking County, Ohio. He was born on 24 Aug 1890 in Starr Township, Hocking County, Ohio. He died on 07 Mar 1971 in Hocking County, Ohio.

More About James Darlington Coakley:
Burial: Forest Rose Cemetery, Lancaster, Fairfield Count, Ohio

More About James Darlington Coakley and Susan Elpha Casto:
Marriage Fact: Married by Reverend T. B. White

James Darlington Coakley and Susan Elpha Casto had the following children:

    i.   VIVIAN L.^{4} COAKLEY was born in 1906 in Ohio.

    ii.   PEARL LEE COAKLEY was born in 1907 in Ohio. She died in 1999.

    iii.   FRANK COAKLEY was born about 1913 in Ohio.

    iv.   THELMA COAKLEY was born about 1916 in Ohio.

More About Joseph Edgar Lattimer:
Living In: 1971 Logan, Hocking County, Ohio

7.   **ROBERT EDWARD**^{3} **CASTO** (George Washington^2, George R.^{1}) was born on 03 Mar 1891 in Cologne District, Mason County, West Virginia. He died on 13 Oct 1958 in Columbus, Franklin County, Ohio. He married **MARY E. FRIEND**. She was born on 17 Feb 1896 in Groveport, Franklin County, Ohio. She died on 13 Nov 1978 in Columbus, Franklin County, Ohio.

More About Robert Edward Casto:
Burial: Forest Lawn Memorial Gardens, Columbus, Franklin County, Ohio
Living In: 1958 Columbus, Franklin County, Ohio
Occupation: 1910 in Logan, Hocking County, Ohio; Odd Jobs Laborer

Occupation: 1930 in Groveport, Franklin County, Ohio; Barber in his own Barber Shop
Occupation: 1942 in Columbus, Franklin County, Ohio; Barber in his own Barber Shop

More About Mary E. Friend:
Burial: Forest Lawn Memorial Gardens, Columbus, Franklin County, Ohio
Living In: 1978 Columbus, Franklin County, Ohio

Notes for Mary E. Friend:
Birth date of February 17, 1896 is from birth record. Social Security death index has birth date of February 18, 1896.

Robert Edward Casto and Mary E. Friend had the following children:

     i.   LILLIAN[4] CASTO was born in 1914. She died in 1930.

     ii.   CLYDE CASTO was born in 1918. He died in 1982.

     iii.   ANNETEPAULINE CASTO was born in 1926. She died in 1995.

8.   **ELSIE MYRTLE[3] CASTO** (George Washington[2], George R.[1]) was born on 15 Jun 1893 in Jackson County, West Virginia. She died on 09 Nov 1957 in Ohio. She married Van Robert Stewart, son of Henry W. Stewart and Deborah McDaniel on 28 May 1910 in Gallia County, Ohio. He was born on 1 Sep 1863 in Mason County, West Virginia. He died on 07 Nov 1939 in Falls Township, Hocking County, Ohio.

More About Elsie Myrtle Casto:
Burial: 12 Nov 1957 in Smith Chapel Cemetery, Logan, Hocking County, Ohio
Living In: 1940 Falls Township, Hocking County, Ohio
Occupation: 1920 ; Hotel Cook, Hocking County, Ohio

Notes for Elsie Myrtle
Casto:
FUNERAL NOTICE
The Athens Messenger, Athens, Athens County, Ohio, Wednesday 13 Nov 1957

Mrs. Stewarts Rites Are Held Tuesday
LOGAN-Funeral services Myrtle Stewart, 64, widow of the Rev. Van R. Stewart, were held at 2 p.m. Tuesday in the Apostolic Gospel Tabernacle.

The Rev. Edwards officiated and music was furnished by Mrs. Kathleen Wells and Mrs. Leona Harden, accompanied by Miss Shirley Sudlow.

Pallbearers were Merl Huffines, Charles Hurst Jr., Larry Yates, David Baker, Harry Casto, and Lawrence Casto. Burial was made in Smith's Chapel Cemetery by the Heinlein funeral home.

More About Van Robert Stewart:
Burial: 10 Nov 1939 in Smith Chapel Cemetery, Logan, Hocking County, Ohio
Occupation: 1900 in Waggener District, Mason County, West Virginia; Day Labor
Occupation: 1910 in Logan, Hocking County, Ohio; Carpenter in Car Shop
Occupation: 1920 in Green Township, Hocking County, Ohio; Hotel Proprietor
Occupation: 1926 in Toledo, Lucas County, Ohio; Car Repair
Occupation: 1928 in Toledo, Lucas County, Ohio; Laborer
Occupation: 1930 in Toledo, Lucas County, Ohio; Salesman
Occupation: 07 Apr 1930 in Toledo, Lucas County, Ohio; Carpenter for Steam Railroad

Notes for Van Robert Stewart:
• Funeral services were held Friday at 2 o'clock at the Iron Street Church for Van Robert Stewart,76, of West Logan, who was killed Tuesday afternoon on U. S. Route 33 near the state highway barns when he was struck by a truck driven by Delmar Walker, Sugar Grove, employee of Ohio Fuel Gas Co. Rev Glenn Lehman McCuneville was in charge of the services and was assisted by Rev. A.F. Pinell, local pastor. Burial was made at Smith Chapel Cemetery by Heinlein Bros. with Clyde Henry and Floyd Stewart, Miranda Castro, John Thomas and Phillip Devol acting as pallbearers. Prosecutor Hubert D. Lappen is conducting an investigation as to the accident, which occurred during a drizzling rain.
  published November 10, 1939

Van Robert Stewart and Elsie Myrtle Casto had the following children:

  i. CORA BEATRICE[4] STEWART was born on 31 Dec 1912 in Logan, Ohio. She died on 21 Jan 2003 in Lancaster, Ohio. She married (1) LUCIUS OAKLEY HARTMANN, son of Henry Andrew Hartmann and Barbara M. Bort on 07 Mar 1942. He was born on 05 May 1907 in Logan, Hocking County, Ohio. He died on 04 Nov 2000 in Lancaster, Ohio. She married (2) ROY MARTIN WOOD, son of Roy C. Wood and Elizabeth Martin on 16 Oct 1930 in Lucas County, Ohio. He was born on 20 Apr 1900 in Antioch, Lake County, Illinois. He died on 13 Nov 1984 in Washington County, Florida.

   More About Cora Beatrice Stewart:
   Burial: 25 Jan 2003 in Maple Grove Cemetery, Lancaster, Fairfield County, Ohio
   Living In: 1935 Athens, Athens County, Ohio
   Living In: 1940 Cora and her two children are living with her mother in Falls Township, Hocking County, Ohio.
   Living In: 2003 Lancaster, Ohio
   Occupation: 1930 in Toledo, Lucas County, Ohio; Restaurant Waitress
   Occupation: 1940 in Falls Township, Hocking County, Ohio; Working in Shoe Factory

  ii. LILLIAN G. STEWART was born on 06 Mar 1916 in Logan, Hocking County, Ohio. She died on 06 Jan 2000 in Sylvania, Lucas County, Ohio. She married PAUL E. UNCLE. He was born on 31 Dec 1910 in Perkins Township, Erie County, Ohio. He died on 20 Feb 1984 in Toledo, Lucas County, Ohio. She married JACK WADE.

   More About Lillian G. Stewart:
   Burial: 10 Jan 2000 in Ottawa Hills Memorial Park, Toledo, Lucas County, Ohio
   Living In: 2000 Toledo, Ohio
   Occupation: Toledo, Lucas County, Ohio; Worked 18 years as a Punch Operator for Toledo Die and Manufacturing

   Notes for Lillian G. Stewart:
   No Children.

  iii. MARIE D. STEWART was born on 04 Sep 1918 in Logan, Ohio. She died on 05 Mar 1940 in Falls Township, Hocking County, Ohio. She married ARTHUR B. HILT. He was born on 16 May 1916 in Hocking County, Ohio. He died on 07 Jun 1963 in Nelsonville, Athens County, Ohio.

   More About Marie D. Stewart:

Burial: 08 Mar 1940 in Smith Chapel Cemetery, Logan, Hocking County, Ohio Cause Of Death: Pulmonary Tuberculosis

iv. ROBERT MCDANIEL STEWART was born on 17 Dec 1920 in Mason County, West Virginia. He died on 18 Jul 1977 in Plant City, Florida. He married (1) PHYLLIS OLENE TUCKER, daughter of William Edward Tucker and Mary Ann Davis on 27 Sep 1940 in Logan, Hocking County, Ohio. She was born on 21 Mar 1922 in Columbus, Ohio. She died on 07 Mar 1991 in Lancaster, Ohio. He married (2) OPAL MAE ANKROM, daughter of Zennie Ankrom and Ethel Hanlin on 14 Feb 1938 in Hocking County, Ohio. She was born on 21 Sep 1920 in Logan, Ohio. She died on 23 Oct 1990 in Circleville, Pickaway County, Ohio.

More About Robert McDaniel Stewart:
Burial: 21 Jul 1977 in Pleasant Grove Cemetery, Durant, Florida
Living In: 1935 Toledo, Lucas County, Ohio
Occupation: 1938 in Hocking County, Ohio; Working in Electrical Refrigeration
Occupation: Apr 1940 in Logan, Hocking County, Ohio; Cab Driver for Cab Company
Occupation: Sep 1940 in South Perry, Hocking County, Ohio; Bar Tender

v. WILLIAM EVERT STEWART was born on 24 Oct 1923 in Hocking County, Ohio. He died on 17 Jan 2009 in Arizona. He married Loretta Jaques, daughter of John Jaques and Retha Nuckles on 26 Nov 1942 in Lucas County, Ohio. She was born on 26 Feb 1925 in Ohio. She died on 15 Dec 1999 in Arizona.

More About William Evert Stewart:
Living In: 2009 Tucson, Pima County, Arizona

vi. ROLLAND RICHARD STEWART was born on 05 Jan 1926 in Ohio. He died on 19 Jan 2005 in Westerville, Delaware County, Ohio. He married MARY LOU KESSLER. She was born on 22 May 1927 in Lancaster, Ohio.

More About Rolland Richard Stewart:
Burial: Resurrection Cemetery, Lewis Center, Delaware County, Ohio
Occupation: 1953 in Columbus, Ohio; Shipping Clerk for Columbus Auto Parts
Military Service: U.S. Navy, World War Two

vii. FRANCES WINNIFRED STEWART was born after 1929 in Ohio. She married FRED R. HOEY. He was born on 10 Nov 1926 in Ohio. He died on 07 Apr 1987 in Wauseon, Fulton County, Ohio. She married (2) RAYMOND PAUL BRESCOL after 07 Apr 1987. He was born in Ohio.

Notes:

Descendants of Abraham E. Johnston

Generation 1

1.   **ABRAHAM E.**[1] **JOHNSTON** was born on 30 Jan 1828 in Taylor County, Virginia. He died on 06 Oct 1886 in Jackson County, West Virginia. He married **SUSAN L. MCMILLAN**. She was born in Sep 1834 in Virginia. She died after 26 Jun 1900.

More About Abraham E. Johnston:
Occupation: 1850 in District 38, Mason County, Virginia; Farmer
Occupation: 1854 in Monongalia County, Virginia; Farmer
Occupation: 1860 in Taylor County, Virginia; Farm Labor
Occupation: 1880 in Cologne District, Mason County, West Virginia; Farm Laborer

More About Susan L. McMillan:
Living In: 1900 With her son, John, in Cologne District, Mason County, West Virginia

Notes for Susan L. McMillan:
James McMillan, Shoe Maker, born about 1785 in Virginia, is living with Abraham and Susan in 1850. Possibly her father.

Abraham E. Johnston and Susan L. McMillan had the following children:

 i. NANCY ISABEL[2] JOHNSTON was born on 26 Dec 1849 in Mason County, Virginia. She died on 30 Jun 1865 in Taylor County, West Virginia.

 ii. JOHN N. JOHNSTON was born in May 1852 in Ohio.

  More About John N. Johnston:
  Living In: 1880 With his parents in Cologne District, Mason County, West Virginia.

 iii. JAMES A. JOHNSTON was born on 14 Sep 1854 in Paulding County, Ohio.

  More About James A. Johnston:
  Living In: 1880 With his parents in Cologne District, Mason County, West Virginia.

2. iv. MARGARET FRANCES JOHNSTON was born on 08 Dec 1856 in Grafton, Taylor County, Virginia. She died on 29 Dec 1928 in Marion Township, Franklin County, Ohio. She married George Washington Casto, son of George R. Casto and Susanna Dewees on 14 Dec 1878 in Mason County, West Virginia. He was born on 09 Aug 1847 in Jackson County, Virginia. He died on 13 Nov 1926 in Falls Township, Hocking County, Ohio.

 v. ARVILLA JOHNSTON was born on 20 Feb 1859 in Taylor County, West Virginia.

 vi. MARY JOHNSTON was born about 1862 in Virginia.

 vii. HESEKIAH ELSWORTH JOHNSTON was born about 1865 in Taylor county, West Virginia. He married Annie Gerutha Seters on 03 May 1884 in Mason County, West Virginia. She was born about 1868 in Meigs County, Ohio.

 viii. HELLEN JOHNSTON was born about 1867 in West Virginia.

 ix. FRANKLIN JOHNSTON was born about 1871 in West Virginia.

x.   WILLIAM JOHNSTON was born about 1873 in West Virginia.

xi.   CLARABELL JOHNSTON was born about 1877 in West Virginia.

Generation 2

2.   MARGARET FRANCES[2] JOHNSTON (Abraham E.[1]) was born on 08 Dec 1856 in Grafton, Taylor County, Virginia. She died on 29 Dec 1928 in Marion Township, Franklin County, Ohio. She married George Washington Casto, son of George R. Casto and Susanna Dewees on 14 Dec 1878 in Mason County, West Virginia. He was born on 09 Aug 1847 in Jackson County, Virginia. He died on 13 Nov 1926 in Falls Township, Hocking County, Ohio.

More About Margaret Frances Johnston:
Burial: 31 Dec 1928 in Oak Grove Cemetery, Logan, Hocking County, Ohio
Cause Of Death: Organic Heart Trouble
Occupation: 1910 in Logan, Hocking County, Ohio; At Home Washerwoman

More About George Washington Casto:
Burial: 15 Nov 1926 in Oak Grove Cemetery, Logan, Hocking County, Ohio
Living In: 1870 With his father and step mother in Union Township, Jackson County, West Virginia.
Occupation: 1870 in Union Township, Jackson County, West Virginia; Farm Laborer
Occupation: 1880 in Cologne District, Mason County, West Virginia; Farm Laborer
Occupation: 1900 in Ripley District, Jackson County, West Virginia; Farmer
Occupation: 1910 in Logan, Hocking County, Ohio; Odd Jobs Laborer
Occupation: 1920 in Falls Township, Hocking County, Ohio; General Farm Laborer

More About George Washington Casto and Margaret Frances Johnston: Marriage
Fact: Married in the home of the Bride's father by B.A. Armstrong, M.G.

George Washington Casto and Margaret Frances Johnston had the following children:

i.   CORA BELLE[3] CASTO was born on 02 Nov 1879 in Mason County, West Virginia. She died on 27 Apr 1956 in Jackson County, West Virginia. She married George Wilman Lathey, son of Joseph W. Lathey and Emma Ward on 26 Feb 1899 in Center Point School House, Jackson County, West Virginia. He was born on 07 May 1878 in Meigs County, Ohio. He died on 16 Dec 1945 in Friendly, Pleasants County, West Virginia.

More About Cora Belle Casto:
Burial: Foster Chapel Cemetery, Evans, Jackson County, West Virginia

ii.   ROSA ELLEN CASTO was born on 28 Aug 1881 in Cottageville, Jackson County, West Virginia. She died on 29 Jan 1976 in Mansfield, Richland County, Ohio. She married (1) KELLEY FREEMAN KAY, son of John Kay and Catherine (unknown) on 20 Jan 1901 in Jackson County, West Virginia. He was born on 22 Dec 1877 in Jackson County, West Virginia. He died on 30 Oct 1918 in Logan, Hocking County, Ohio. She married (2) FRANK ELMER WOLFE, son of David Wolfe and Mary Mowery on 20 Feb 1926 in Franklin County, ohio. He was born on 19 May 1884 in Hocking county, Ohio. He died on 11 Jun 1950 in Cleveland, Cuyahoga County, Ohio. She married (3) ALBERT BURKHART, son of Fred Burkhart and Mary Haggi on 21 Apr 1939 in Perry County, Ohio. He was born on 30 Jan 1896 in Ohio. He died on 16 Dec 1968 in Columbus, Franklin County, Ohio.

More About Rosa Ellen Casto:
Burial: Oak Grove Cemetery, Logan, Hocking County, Ohio
Living In: 1976 Last residence was in Logan, Hocking County, Ohio

3.   MIRANDA NICHOLAS CASTO was born on 09 Aug 1883 in Cottageville, Jackson
County, West Virginia. He died on 27 Jan 1971 in Hocking County, Ohio. He
married (1) BESSIE LOUESA RUBLE, daughter of James Merley Ruble and Mary
Jane Poling on 29 Jan 1907 in Hocking County, Ohio. She was born on 03 Jan
1883 in Falls Township, Hocking County, Ohio. She died in 1955. He married (2)
XEMA BRAY VEST, daughter of Joseph Vest and Clara M. Bray on 07 Jun 1958 in
Hocking County, Ohio. She was born on 26 Mar 1889 in Benton Township,
Hocking County, Ohio. She died on 10 Apr 1987 in Logan, Hocking County, Ohio.

More About Miranda Nicholas Casto:
Burial: Oak Grove Cemetery, Logan, Hocking County,
Ohio
Living In: 1907   Logan, Ohio
Living In: 1942   Logan, Ohio
Living In: 1971   Logan, Ohio
Occupation: 1942; Working at Hocking Valley Brick
Company
Occupation: Minister

Notes for Miranda Nicholas Casto:
World War One and World War Two draft registrations give middle name
as Nichola.

4.   SUSAN ELPHA CASTO was born on 27 May 1886 in Jackson County, West Virginia.
She married (1) JAMES DARLINGTON COAKLEY, son of Augustus Coakley and
Margaret Joy on 29 May 1903 in Hocking County, Ohio. He was born on 27 Dec
1877 in York Township, Athens County, Ohio. He died on 01 Feb 1954 in
Lancaster, Ohio. She married (2) JOSEPH EDGAR LATTIMER, son of David Lattimer
and Catherine Willison on 30 Dec 1919 in Hocking County, Ohio. He was born
on 24 Aug 1890 in Starr Township, Hocking County, Ohio. He died on 07 Mar
1971 in Hocking County, Ohio.

5.   A. J. CASTO was born on 06 Oct 1888 in Jackson County, West Virginia. She
died before 16 Jun 1900.

Notes for A. J. Casto:
Birth date and gender are from birth record.

6.   ROBERT EDWARD CASTO was born on 03 Mar 1891 in Cologne District, Mason County,
West Virginia. He died on 13 Oct 1958 in Columbus, Franklin County, Ohio. He
married MARY E. FRIEND. She was born on 17 Feb 1896 in Groveport, Franklin County,
Ohio. She died on 13 Nov 1978 in Columbus, Franklin County, Ohio.

More About Robert Edward Casto:
Burial: Forest Lawn Memorial Gardens, Columbus, Franklin County,
Ohio Living In: 1958 Columbus, Franklin County, Ohio
Occupation: 1910 in Logan, Hocking County, Ohio; Odd Jobs Laborer
Occupation: 1930 in Groveport, Franklin County, Ohio; Barber in his own
Barber Shop
Occupation: 1942 in Columbus, Franklin County, Ohio; Barber in his own Barber

Shop

vii.	ELSIE MYRTLE CASTO was born on 15 Jun 1893 in Jackson County, West Virginia. She died on 09 Nov 1957 in Ohio. She married Van Robert Stewart, son of Henry W. Stewart and Deborah McDaniel on 28 May 1910 in Gallia County, Ohio. He was born on 01 Sep 1863 in Mason County, West Virginia. He died on 07 Nov 1939 in Falls Township, Hocking County, Ohio.

More About Elsie Myrtle Casto:
Burial: 12 Nov 1957 in Smith Chapel Cemetery, Logan, Hocking County, Ohio Living In: 1940 Falls Township, Hocking County, Ohio
Occupation: 1920; Hotel Cook, Hocking County, Ohio

Notes for Elsie Myrtle
Casto:
FUNERAL NOTICE
The Athens Messenger, Athens, Athens County, Ohio, Wednesday 13 Nov 1957

Mrs. Stewarts Rites Are Held Tuesday
LOGAN-Funeral services Myrtle Stewart, 64, widow of the Rev. Van R. Stewart, were held at 2 p.m. Tuesday in the Apostolic Gospel Tabernacle.

The Rev. Edwards officiated and music was furnished by Mrs. Kathleen Wells and Mrs. Leona Harden, accompanied by Miss Shirley Sudlow.

Pallbearers were Merl Huffines, Charles Hurst Jr., Larry Yates, David Baker, Harry Casto, and Lawrence Casto. Burial was made in Smith's Chapel Cemetery by the Heinlein funeral home.

viii.	LESTIE GERTRUDE CASTO was born on 08 Aug 1896 in Jackson County, West Virginia. She married (1) JAMES EVERETT STEWART, son of Van Robert Stewart and Cora B. Swan on 14 Jun 1913 in Hocking County, Ohio. He was born on 25 Jan 1891 in Silex, Lincoln County, Missouri. He died in Oct 1963 in West Virginia. She married (2) ABRAM BARBER, son of Jared Barber and Alice H. Walls on 04 Aug 1923 in Franklin County, Ohio. He was born on 14 Jul 1895 in Mundy, Hocking County, Ohio. He died on 25 Jul 1964 in Nelsonville, Athens County, Ohio.

More About Lestie Gertrude Casto:
Living In: 1913 Logan, Hocking County, Ohio
Living In: 27 Jan 1920 living as Gertrude Casto with Van Robert Stewart and his family in Green Township, Hocking County, Ohio.
Living In: 1923 Franklin County, Ohio
Occupation: 14 Jun 1913 in Logan, Hocking County, Ohio; Dining Room Girl
Occupation: 1920 in Green Township, Hocking County, Ohio; Cook in hotel Owned by Van Robert Stewart

Descendants of Hutchinson McDaniel

Generation 1

1. **HUTCHINSON**[1] **MCDANIEL** was born on 04 Aug 1807 in Virginia. He died on 06 Jan 1875 in Mason County, West Virginia. He married Hannah Johnson, daughter of Robert Johnson and Anna Greenlee on 23 Mar 1833 in Mason County, Virginia. She was born in 1818 in Virginia. She died on 30 Nov 1870 in Mason County, West Virginia.

More About Hutchinson McDaniel:
Burial: Pioneer Cemetery, Point Pleasant, Mason County, West Virginia
Occupation: 1850 in District 38, Mason County, Virginia; Farmer
Occupation: 1860 in District 1, Mason County, Virginia; Farmer
Occupation: 1870 in Point Pleasant, Mason County, West Virginia; Jailor

Hutchinson McDaniel and Hannah Johnson had the following children:

    i. VAN D.[2] MCDANIEL was born about 1836 in Virginia. He died on 10 Sep 1863 in Point Pleasant, West Virginia. He married Frances E. Ball, daughter of Thomas Ball and Julia Hogg on 21 Feb 1859 in Mason County, Virginia. She was born in 1839 in Virginia. She died in 1916 in West Virginia.

        More About Van D. McDaniel:
        Burial: Pioneer Cemetery, Point Pleasant, Mason County, West Virginia
        Cause Of Death: Camp Dysentery
        Military Service: Bet. 09 Oct 1862-10 Sep 1863 in Company C, 13th West Virginia Infantry, U.S. Army

        Notes for Van D. McDaniel:
        Died of disease while serving in U.S. Army.
        Enrolled in 13th West Virginia Infantry on August 15, 1862 and mustered into service on October 9, 1862.
        Served as Captain of company C, 13th West Virginia Infantry
        U. S. Army records give his age as 26 on October 9, 1862

2.   ii. WILLIAM MCDANIEL was born on 25 Sep 1839 in Mason County, Virginia. He died between 04 Jun 1870-06 Jun 1900. He married Elizabeth Stewart, daughter of William Stewart and Martha Ann Van Sickle on 19 Dec 1861 in Pleasant Flats, Mason County, Virginia. She was born on 30 Jan 1839 in Mason County, Virginia. She died on 27 May 1926 in Robinson District, Mason County, West Virginia.

3.   iii. DEBORAH MCDANIEL was born on 30 Jul 1843 in Mason County, Virginia. She died on 17 Mar 1900 in Mason County, West Virginia. She married Henry W. Stewart, son of William Stewart and Martha Ann Van Sickle on 15 Sep 1862 in Point Pleasant, Mason County, Virginia. He was born on 16 Dec 1830 in Mason County, Virginia. He died on 30 Aug 1905 in West Columbia, Mason County, West Virginia.

4.   iv. MARY ANN MCDANIEL was born on 25 Jul 1846 in Mason County, Virginia. She died on 18 Jan 1928 in Pike County, Missouri. She married John P. Wood, son of George Wood and Mary Ann (unknown) on 27 Feb 1866 in Point Pleasant, Mason County, West Virginia. He was born on 12 Feb 1833 in Nelson County, Virginia. He died on 14 Oct 1890 in Pike County, Missouri.

    v.   OLEVIA MCDANIEL was born on 15 Dec 1849 in Virginia. She died on 29 Jul 1861 in Virginia.

More About Olevia McDaniel:
Burial: Pioneer Cemetery, Point Pleasant, Mason County, West Virginia

v.   vi. ROBERT WESLEY MCDANIEL was born on 08 Mar 1852 in Virginia. He died on 17 Apr 1924 in Bowie, Montague County, Texas. He married Lucinda P. Burkholder, daughter of Alexander Burkholder and Harriet Penn about 1871. She was born on 08 May 1853 in Virginia. She died on 02 Sep 1940 in Bowie, Montague County, Texas.

JOHN MCDANIEL was born on 11 Aug 1856 in Mason County, Virginia. He died on 11 Aug 1861 in Mason County, Virginia.

More About John McDaniel:
Burial: Pioneer Cemetery, Point Pleasant, Mason County, West Virginia

PATSY J. MCDANIEL was born about 1859 in Virginia.

JESSIE B. MCDANIEL was born about 1863 in Virginia.

Generation 2

2.   WILLIAM^2 MCDANIEL (Hutchinson^1) was born on 25 Sep 1839 in Mason County, Virginia. He died between 04 Jun 1870 and 06 Jun 1900. He married Elizabeth Stewart, daughter of William Stewart and Martha Ann Van Sickle on 19 Dec 1861 in Pleasant Flats, Mason County, Virginia. She was born on 30 Jan 1839 in Mason County, Virginia. She died on 27 May 1926 in Robinson District, Mason County, West Virginia.

More About William McDaniel:
Occupation: 1870 in Cuivre Township, Pike County, Missouri; Farmer

Notes for William McDaniel:
Probably died in Missouri between June 4, 1870 and December 1, 1879.

More About Elizabeth Stewart:
Burial: 29 May 1926 in Stewart Cemetery, Mason County, West
Virginia
Living In: Dec 1879 Mason County, West Virginia
Living In: 1900 As a widow Robinson Distict, Mason County, West Virginia.
Living In: 1910 As a widow Robinson District, Mason County, West Virginia.
Living In: 1920 With her grand daughter, Clara, and her family in Robinson District, Mason County, West Virginia.
Occupation: 1900 in Robinson District, Mason County, West Virginia; Farmer

Notes for Elizabeth Stewart:
Death certificate gives burial place as Stewart Cemetery. Headstone is present in Lone Oak Cemetery.

Elizabeth was present at Madaline's wedding to give permission for Madaline to get married but there is no mention of Madaline's father.

William McDaniel and Elizabeth Stewart had the following child:

    i. MADALINE[3] MCDANIEL was born on 09 Dec 1862 in Mason County, Virginia. She died on 14 Oct 1954 in Point Pleasant, Mason County, West Virginia. She married William F. Stewart, son of John B. Stewart and Elizabeth M. (unknown) on 01 Dec 1879 in Point Pleasant, Mason County, West Virginia. He was born in 1855 in Jefferson County, Kentucky. He died in 1882.

    More About Madaline McDaniel:
    Burial: 17 Oct 1954 in Lone Oak Cemetery, Point Pleasant, Mason County, West Virginia
    Cause Of Death: Uremia
    Living In: 1900 Madaline and her daughter are living with her mother in Robinson District, Mason County, West Virginia.
    Living In: 1910 With her mother in Robinson District, Mason County, West Virginia.
    Living In: 1920 With her daughter, Clara, and her family in Robinson District, Mason County, West Virginia.

3. **DEBORAH[2] MCDANIEL** (Hutchinson[1]) was born on 30 Jul 1843 in Mason County, Virginia. She died on 17 Mar 1900 in Mason County, West Virginia. She married Henry W. Stewart, son of William Stewart and Martha Ann Van Sickle on 15 Sep 1862 in Point Pleasant, Mason County, Virginia. He was born on 16 Dec 1830 in Mason County, Virginia. He died on 30 Aug 1905 in West Columbia, Mason County, West Virginia.

More About Deborah McDaniel:
Burial: Stewart Cemetery, Mason County, West Virginia

More About Henry W. Stewart:
Burial: 02 Sep 1905 in Stewart Cemetery, Mason County, West Virginia
Cause Of Death: Brights Disease
Living In: 1860 With his parents in District 1, Mason County, Virginia
Occupation: 1860 in District 1, Mason County, Virginia; Farmer
Occupation: 1870 in Cuivre Township, Pike County, Missouri; Farmer
Occupation: 1880 in Cuivre Township, Pike County, Missouri; Farmer
Occupation: 1900 in Robinson District, Mason County, West Virginia; Farmer

Henry W. Stewart and Deborah McDaniel had the following children:

    i. VAN ROBERT[3] STEWART was born on 01 Sep 1863 in Mason County, West Virginia. He died on 07 Nov 1939 in Falls Township, Hocking County, Ohio. He married (1) ELSIE MYRTLE CASTO, daughter of George Washington Casto and Margaret Frances Johnston on 28 May 1910 in Gallia County, Ohio. She was born on 15 Jun 1893 in Jackson County, West Virginia. She died on 09 Nov 1957 in Ohio. He married (2) CORA B. SWAN, daughter of A . Swan on 24 Oct 1889 in Pike County, Missouri. She was born about 1871 in Missouri. She died on 28 Dec 1896 in Lincoln County, Missouri. He married (3) MARY WEBER on 08 Aug 1897 in Lincoln County, Missouri. She died before 07 Jun 1900.

    More About Van Robert Stewart:
    Burial: 10 Nov 1939 in Smith Chapel Cemetery, Logan, Hocking County, Ohio
    Occupation: 1900 in Waggener District, Mason County, West Virginia; Day Labor
    Occupation: 1910 in Logan, Hocking County, Ohio; Carpenter in Car Shop
    Occupation: 1920 in Green Township, Hocking County, Ohio; Hotel Proprietor
    Occupation: 1926 in Toledo, Lucas County, Ohio; Car Repair
    Occupation: 1928 in Toledo, Lucas County, Ohio; Laborer

Occupation: 1930 in Toledo, Lucas County, Ohio; Salesman
Occupation: 07 Apr 1930 in Toledo, Lucas County, Ohio; Carpenter for
Steam Railroad

Notes for Van Robert Stewart:
• Funeral services were held Friday at 2 o'clock at the Iron Street Church for Van
Robert Stewart,76, of West Logan, who was killed Tuesday afternoon on U. S.
Route 33 near the state highway barns when he was struck by a truck driven by
Delmar Walker, Sugar Grove, employee of Ohio Fuel Gas Co. Rev Glenn
Lehman McCuneville was in charge of the services and was assisted by Rev.
A.F. Pinell, local pastor. Burial was made at Smith Chapel Cemetery by Heinlein
Bros. with Clyde Henry and Floyd Stewart, Miranda Castro, John Thomas and
Phillip Devol acting as pallbearers. Prosecutor Hubert D. Lappen is conducting an
investigation as to the accident, which occurred during a drizzling rain.
           published November 10, 1939
----

ii.   ANDREW JOHNSON STEWART was born on 09 Jan 1866 in Mason County, West
      Virginia.

iii. WILLIAM HUDSON STEWART was born on 26 Feb 1868 in Calumet Township, Pike
      County, Missouri. He died on 18 Jul 1915 in Calumet Township, Pike County,
      Missouri. He married Martha Ellen Stilffler on 10 Mar 1889 in Ashley Township,
      Pike County, Missouri. She was born on 28 May 1873 in Wisconsin. She died on
      22 Oct 1948 in Elsberry, Lincoln County, Missouri.

      More About William Hudson Stewart:
      Burial: 19 Jul 1915 in Oak Ridge Cemetery, Lincoln County,
      Missouri Cause Of Death: Hit by falling scaffold.
      Occupation: 1900 in Buffalo Township, Pike County, Missouri; Day Laborer
      Occupation: 1910 in Hurricane Township, Lincoln County, Missouri; Farm Laborer

      Notes for William Hudson Stewart:
      Death Certificate gives place of death as Calumet Township, Pike County, Missouri.

      Injury leading to his death occured in Dameron, Lincoln County, Missouri.
      ----

iv.   VIOLA B. STEWART was born on 25 Dec 1869 in Missouri. She died on 17 Jun 1959 in
      Clifton, Mason County, West Virginia. She married (1) JOHN LEONARD WEBBER before
      27 Apr 1893 in Missouri. He was born on 16 May 1858. He died on 27 Jan 1941. She
      married (2) GEORGE HAMILTON STEWART, son of Jesse Franklin Stewart and Sarah
      Catherine Johnson on 28 May 1900 in New Cumberland, Hancock County, West
      Virginia. He was born on 27 Dec 1875 in Mason County, West Virginia. He died on
      27 Sep 1945 in Athens, Athens County, Ohio.

      More About Viola B. Stewart:
      Burial: 20 Jun 1959 in Letart Falls Cemetery, Letart Falls, Meigs County,
      Ohio
      Cause Of Death: Bronchial Pneumonia

v.   ALVERETTA STEWART was born about 1872 in Missouri.

vi.   JOHN MACK STEWART was born on 14 Jul 1875 in Pike County, Missouri. He died on 27 Apr 1937 in West Columbia, Mason County, West Virginia. He married (1) DORA CLEMENTINE LEWIS, daughter of Isaac J. Lewis and Elizabeth Wetzel on 18 Oct 1899 in Mason County, West Virginia. She was born on 09 May 1880 in New Garden Township, Wayne County, Indiana. She died on 24 Jul 1942 in Charleston, Kanawha County, West Virginia. He married (2) ELIZABETH REBECCA VAN MATRE, daughter of David Van Matre and Harriett Rebecca Lewis on 25 Apr 1908 in Hartford, Mason County, West virginia. She was born on 11 Feb 1889 in West Virginia. She died on 15 Apr 1979 in Meigs County, Ohio.

More About John Mack Stewart:
Burial: 29 Apr 1937 in Graham Cemetery, Mason County, West Virginia
Cause Of Death: Polycythemia
Living In: 1900 Living, with his wife Dora, in the household of his father in Mason County, West Virginia
Occupation: 1900 in Robinson District, Mason County, West Virginia; Farmer
Occupation: 1910 in Logan, Hocking County, Ohio; Car Carpenter
Occupation: 1920 in Waggener District, Mason County, West Virginia; Car Repair in Car Shop
Occupation: 1930 in Waggener District, Mason County, West Virginia; Carpenter in Car Shop

Notes for John Mack Stewart:
World War One draft registration and death certificate have his middle name as "Mack".

vii.   HENRY EGBERT STEWART was born on 15 Nov 1878 in West Columbia, Mason County, West Virginia. He died on 21 Jan 1951 in Gallipolis, Gallia County, Ohio. He married Eva Louella Thompson, daughter of Green Thompson and Sarah Crookham on 26 Sep 1906 in Clifton, Mason County, West Virginia. She was born on 01 Jun 1886 in West Virginia. She died on 16 Aug 1957 in West Columbia, Mason County, West Virginia.

More About Henry Egbert Stewart:
Burial: 24 Jan 1951 in Suncrest Cemetery, Point Pleasant, Mason County, West Virginia
Cause Of Death: Myocardial Infarction
Living In: 1900 With his brother, Van R. Stewart, in Waggener District, Mason County, West Virginia.
Living In: 1918   West Columbia, Mason County, West Virginia
Living In: 1942   West Columbia, Mason County, West Virginia
Occupation: 1910 in West Columbia, Mason County, West Virginia; Coal Miner
Occupation: 1918 in Hebron, Ohio; Car Carpenter for K.M. Railroad
Occupation: 1920 in Waggener District, Mason County, West Virginia; House Carpenter
Occupation: 1930 in Waggener District, Mason County, West Virginia; Carpenter in Car Factory
Occupation: 1940 in Letart Township, Meigs County, Ohio; Farm Labor
Occupation: 1942 in Middleport, Meigs County, Ohio; Working for N.Y.C. Railroad
Occupation: Truck Gardening

Notes for Henry Egbert Stewart:
Lived in West Columbia, Mason county, West Virginia at the time of his death. Died

in Gallipolis, Ohio while in Holzer hospital.

World War One and World War Two draft registrations give date of birth as
November 15, 1878. Death certificate and headstone have year of birth as 1877.

----

viii.   CLYDE WYATT STEWART was born on 19 Jul 1881 in Pike County, Missouri. He died on
13 Jul 1969 in Clifton, Mason County, West Virginia. He married (1) MARTHA (MATTIE) A.
KEARNS, daughter of Jesse Kearns and Martha M. Stewart on 11 Jun 1902 in Mason
County, West Virginia. She was born on 04 Jun 1885 in Mason County, West Virginia.
She died on 06 Nov 1919 in West Columbia, Mason County, West Virginia. He
married (2) ANNA LEE RODGERS, daughter of John Michael Rodgers and Elizabeth
Francis Stewart on 18 Sep 1920 in Point Pleasant, Mason County, West Virginia. She
was born on 12 May 1895 in Old Town, Mason County, West Virginia. He married (3)
CATHERINE VIRGINIA VAN METER, daughter of Winfield Scott Van Meter and Margaret
May Russell on 02 May 1945 in Gallia County, Ohio. She was born on 23 Jan 1884 in
West Columbia, Mason County, Ohio. She died on 17 Aug 1966 in Middleport, Meigs
County, Ohio.

More About Clyde Wyatt Stewart:
Burial: 16 Jul 1969 in Riverview Cemetery, Middleport, Meigs County,
Ohio Cause Of Death: Coronary Occlusion and Pulmonary Tuberculosis
Living In: 1918 West Columbia, Mason County, West Virginia
Living In: 1942 Middleport, Meigs County, Ohio
Occupation: 1910 in Logan, Hocking County, Ohio; Car Carpenter
Occupation: 1918 in Hobson, Meigs County, Ohio; Car Carpenter for H.M.
Railroad
Occupation: 1920 in Waggener District, Mason County, West Virginia; Car
Repairer at Car Works
Occupation: 1930 in Waggener District, Mason County, West Virginia; Car
Repairer at Railroad Shop
Occupation: 1942 in Hobson, Meigs County, Ohio; Working for New York
Central Railroad
Occupation: 1945 in Middleport, Ohio;
Welder

Notes for Clyde Wyatt Stewart:

CLIFTON - Clyde W. Stewart, 87, Clifton, died early Sunday at the home of a
sister, Mrs. Maude Vanmeter, Clifton.

Born in Missouri, he was a son of the late Henry and Deborah McDaniel Stewart.

Surviving are three daughters, Mrs. Mabel Hutton, West Jefferson, Ohio, Mrs. Irene
Wells, Pomeroy, and Mrs. Violet Ray, Columbus, Ga.; three sons, Floyd and Almo
Stewart, both of Toledo, and Leo of West Columbia; seven stepsons, Tommy, Lonnie,
John, Marvin and Clayton Smith and Franklin and Edgar Workman; two sisters, Mrs.
Maude VanMeter, Clifton and Mrs. Julia VanMeter, West Columbia.

Funeral services will be held Wednesday at 3 p.m. in West Columbia United
Methodist Church with the Rev. O.H. Carder and the Rev. Eddie Boyer
officiating. Burial will be in Riverview Cemetery in Middleport.

Friends may call at Foglesong Funeral Home Tuesday 2 to 4 p.m. and 7 to 9 p.m. The body will be taken to the church one hour before the funeral.

Athens Messenger
July 14, 1969.

Middle name is from World War Two draft registration.
----

ix. MAUD B. STEWART was born on 23 Sep 1884 in Pike County, Missouri. She died on 19 Mar 1985 in Clifton, Mason County, West Virginia. She married GEORGE STEWART. He was born in Point Pleasant, Mason County, West Virginia. She married (2) HARRY DANIEL V AN METER, son of Leonard Van Meter and Elizabeth Edwards on 25 Dec 1907 in Clifton, Mason County, West Virginia. He was born on 07 Jul 1874 in Mason County, West Virginia. He died on 02 May 1946 in Clifton, Mason County, West Virginia.

More About Maud B. Stewart:
Burial: Graham Cemetery, Mason County, West Virginia
Living In: 1900 With her brother, Van R. Stewart, in Waggener District, Mason County, West Virginia.

Notes for Maud B. Stewart:
Social Security death index gives birth date as September 23, 1883 and spells first name as Maud. Marriage licence indicates a birth year of 1883. 1900 U.S. Census gives September 1884 as birth date.
Headstone gives date of birth as September 23, 1884. First name is spelled Maud when she signs her husband's death certificate. First name is spelled Maud on her husband's World War One draft registration. First name is spelled Maud on her headstone.
----

x. JULIA F. STEWART was born on 03 Jan 1887 in Pike County, Missouri. She died in May 1972 in Mason County, West Virginia. She married Howard D. Van Matre, son of David Van Matre and Harriett Rebecca Lewis on 26 Aug 1905 in Point Pleasant, Mason County, West Virginia. He was born on 17 Aug 1883 in Mason County, West Virginia. He died on 06 Feb 1957 in West Columbia, Mason County, West Virginia.

More About Julia F. Stewart:
Burial: Graham Cemetery, Mason County, West Virginia

4   MARY ANN[2] MCDANIEL (Hutchinson[1]) was born on 25 Jul 1846 in Mason County, Virginia. She died on 18 Jan 1928 in Pike County, Missouri. She married John P. Wood, son of George Wood and Mary Ann (unknown) on 27 Feb 1866 in Point Pleasant, Mason County, West Virginia. He was born on 12 Feb 1833 in Nelson County, Virginia. He died on 14 Oct 1890 in Pike County, Missouri.

More About Mary Ann McDaniel:
Burial: Antioch Cemetery, Cyrene, Pike County, Missouri

More About John P. Wood:
Burial: Antioch Cemetery, Cyrene, Pike County, Missouri
Occupation: 1866 in Mason County, West Virginia; Farmer
Occupation: 1870 in Cuivre Township, Pike County, Missouri; Farmer
Occupation: 1880 in Cuivre Township, Pike County, Missouri; Farmer

John P. Wood and Mary Ann McDaniel had the following children:

    i.   ADA BELL[3] WOOD was born about 1867 in Missouri.

    ii.   ELMORE WOOD was born about 1872 in Missouri.

v.   **ROBERT WESLEY[2] MCDANIEL** (Hutchinson[1]) was born on 08 Mar 1852 in Virginia. He died on 17 Apr 1924 in Bowie, Montague County, Texas. He married Lucinda P. Burkholder, daughter of Alexander Burkholder and Harriet Penn about 1871. She was born on 08 May 1853 in Virginia. She died on 02 Sep 1940 in Bowie, Montague County, Texas.

More About Robert Wesley McDaniel:
Burial: 18 Apr 1924 in Elmwood Cemetery, Bowie, Montague County,Texas
Cause Of Death: Cancer
Living In: 1880 Precinct 3, Cooke County, Texas
Living In: 1900 Bowie, Montague County, Texas
Occupation: Merchant

More About Lucinda P. Burkholder:
Burial: 03 Sep 1940 in Elmwood Cemetery, Bowie, Montague County,Texas
Living In: 1940 Bowie, Montague County, Texas

Robert Wesley McDaniel and Lucinda P. Burkholder had the following children:

    i CHARLES[3] MCDANIEL was born about 1872 in Missouri.

    ii DORA MCDANIEL was born about 1874 in Missouri.

    iii ERNEST G. MCDANIEL was born on 18 Dec 1874 in Missouri. He died on 06 Aug 1896 in Texas.

        More About Ernest G. McDaniel:
        Burial: Elmwood Cemetery, Bowie, Montague County,Texas

    iv Myrtle McDaniel was born about 1876 in Missouri

    v OLIVIA MCDANIEL was born about 1880 in Texas.

    vi VIRGIL O. MCDANIEL was born on 01 Mar 1884. He died on 24 Oct 1895 in Texas.

        More About Virgil O. McDaniel:
        Burial: Elmwood Cemetery, Bowie, Montague County,Texas

    vii KATEY MCDANIEL was born in Sep 1886 in Texas.

    viii JAMES MONROE MCDANIEL was born on 06 Apr 1888 in Texas. He died on 05 Feb 1963 in Bowie, Montague County, Texas.

More About James Monroe McDaniel:
Burial: 07 Feb 1963 in Elmwood Cemetery, Bowie, Montague County,Texas
Living In: 1940 With his mother in Bowie, Montague County, Texas.

ix.   OPAL MCDANIEL was born in Oct 1896 in Texas.

x.   ROBERT W. MCDANIEL was born on 06 Oct 1898 in Texas. He died on 11 Jan 1901 in Texas.

More About Robert W. McDaniel:
Burial: Elmwood Cemetery, Bowie, Montague County,Texas

Notes:

Descendants of Samuel Van Sickle

Generation 1

1. **Samuel**[1] **Van Sickle** . He married **Sarah Thompson**.

Samuel Van Sickle and Sarah Thompson had the following children:

2.   i. Anthony[2] Van Sickle was born about 1770 in New Jersey. He died on 29 Sep 1815 in Mason County, Virginia. He married (1) Rebecca Van Meter, daughter of Henry Van Meter and Martha Moore on 29 Apr 1789 in Green County, Pennsylvania. She was born in Green County, Pennsylvania. She died on 28 Dec 1810 in Mason County, Virginia. He married (2) Zilpha Hubbell, daughter of Abijah Hubbell on 06 Jun 1811 in Gallia County, Ohio. She died on 21 Nov 1857 in Meigs County, Ohio.

          ii Zachariah Van Sickle.

          iii Rebecca Van Sickle.

          iv Christine Van Sickle was born in Pennsylvania. She died in Mason County, Virginia. She married Henry Van Meter. He was born in Jun 1773 in Pennsylvania. He died on 13 Dec 1857 in Mason County, Virginia.

Generation 2

2 **Anthony**[2] **Van Sickle** (Samuel[1]) was born about 1770 in New Jersey. He died on 29 Sep 1815 in Mason County, Virginia. He married (1) **Rebecca Van Meter**, daughter of Henry Van Meter and Martha Moore on 29 Apr 1789 in Green County, Pennsylvania. She was born in Green County, Pennsylvania. She died on 28 Dec 1810 in Mason County, Virginia. He married (2) **Zilpha Hubbell**, daughter of Abijah Hubbell on 06 Jun 1811 in Gallia County, Ohio. She died on 21 Nov 1857 in Meigs County, Ohio.

More About Anthony Van Sickle:
Burial: Point Pleasant, Virginia
Military Service: Mason County, Virginia; Captain of Anthony Van Sickle's Mason County Riflemen in War of 1812.

Anthony Van Sickle and Rebecca Van Meter had the following children:

          i.   Henry[3] Van Sickle was born in 1793 in Green County, Pennsylvania. He died on 12 Nov 1863. He married Rachel Swan.

          ii.   Jesse Van Sickle was born in 1796 in Green County, Pennsylvania.

          iii. Hannah Van Sickle was born in 1798 in Mason County, Virginia.

          iv.   Anthony Van Sickle was born in 1800 in Mason County, Virginia.

4   v.   Abraham Van Sickle was born on 21 Oct 1802 in Mason County, Virginia. He died on 05 Feb 1873. He married Mary Riffle. She died after 21 Jun 1870.

5   vi.   Samuel Van Sickle was born about 1803 in Virginia.

6   vii. Martha Ann Van Sickle was born on 15 Oct 1804 in Mason County, Virginia. She died on 02 Feb 1877 in Mason County, West Virginia. She married William Stewart, son of Robert Stewart and Catherine Aleshire on 13 Sep 1823 in Mason County, Virginia. He was born on 09 Sep 1802 in Bath County, Virginia. He died on 16 Jul

1882 in Mason County, West Virginia.

viii.   JOHN VAN SICKLE was born in 1807 in Mason County, Virginia.

ix.   JOSEPH VAN SICKLE was born on 12 Feb 1809 in Mason County, Virginia. He died on 13 Aug 1884 in Farmington, St. Francois County, Missouri. He married (1) MARY MAHALA HINKLE, daughter of Gideon Hinkle and Rhoda Jane Allen on 26 Dec 1833. She was born about 1815. He married (2) SARAH RICKERT in 1836. She was born on 02 Nov 1816 in Virginia. She died on 16 Dec 1883 in Farmington, St. Francois County, Missouri.

More About Joseph Van Sickle:
Burial: 14 Aug 1884 in Farmington, St. Francois County, Missouri
Occupation: ; Minister

x.   ELI VAN SICKLE was born in 1810 in Mason County, Virginia.

Anthony Van Sickle and Zilpha Hubbell had the following children:

11.   REBECCAH VAN SICKLE was born on 25 Apr 1812. She died on 29 Apr 1812.

12.   ABIJAH VAN SICKLE was born on 15 Apr 1813.

13.   MARY VAN SICKLE was born on 01 Jan 1816. She died on 29 Apr 1854.

Generation 3

3.   **ABRAHAM**[3] **VAN SICKLE** (Anthony[2], Samuel[1]) was born on 21 Oct 1802 in Mason County, Virginia. He died on 05 Feb 1873. He married **MARY RIFFLE**. She died after 21 Jun 1870.

More About Abraham Van Sickle:
Occupation: 1850 in District 38, Mason County, Virginia; Farmer
Occupation: 1860 in District 1, Mason County, Virginia; Farmer
Occupation: 1870 in Robinson Township, Mason County, West Virginia

Abraham Van Sickle and Mary Riffle had the following children:

i.   ANTHONY[4] VAN SICKLE was born in 1832 in Virginia. He married Magdalen Ann Riffle, daughter of Johnathon Riffle and Nancy (unknown) on 14 Feb 1854 in Marshall County, Virginia. She was born in 1827.

ii.   GEORGE V AN SICKLE was born in 1835 in Mason County, Virginia. He died on 06 May 1897 in Old Town, Mason County, West virginia. He married LUCY (UNKNOWN).

iii.   LEWIS J. VAN SICKLE was born on 16 Oct 1838 in Virginia. He died on 30 Dec 1907 in Seymour, Wayne County, Iowa.

iv.

More About Lewis J. Van Sickle:
Burial: 30 Dec 1907 in Seymour, Wayne County, Iowa

v.   ELI WASHINGTON VAN SICKLE was born on 16 Oct 1838 in Virginia. He died in 1910 in Mason County. WEest virginia. He married Mary Margaret Eckard, daughter of Thomas Eckard and Elizabeth Riffle on 02 Jul 1895 in Point Pleasant, Mason County, West Virginia. She was born on 06 Jun 1847 in Mason County, Virginia.

She died on 11 Sep 1928 in Beech Hill, Mason County, West Virginia.

More About Eli Washington Van Sickle:
Burial: Pine Grove Cemetery, Mason County, West Virginia

CATHERINE VAN SICKLE was born about 1844 in Virginia. She married GEORGE WASHINGTON FOGELSONG.

SAMUEL VAN SICKLE was born on 25 Jan 1847 in Mason County, Virginia. He died on 31 Dec 1936 in Beech Hill, Mason County, West Virginia. He married REBECCA JANE BIRCHFIELD. She was born on 05 Oct 1850 in Wyoming County, Virginia. She died on 27 Dec 1936 in Beech Hill, Mason County, West Virginia.

More About Samuel Van Sickle:
Burial: 01 Jan 1937 in Van Sickle Cemetery, Mason County, West Virginia

DANIEL C. VAN SICKLE was born about 1850 in Virginia.

iv.   **SAMUEL**[3] **VAN SICKLE** (Anthony[2], Samuel[1]) was born about 1803 in Virginia.

More About Samuel Van Sickle:
Occupation: 1880 in Robinson District, Mason County, West Virginia; Farmer

Samuel Van Sickle had the following children:

MARY[4] VAN SICKLE was born about 1855 in Virginia.

CATHERINE VAN SICKLE was born about 1874 in West Virginia.

STEPHEN VAN SICKLE was born about 1876 in West Virginia.

SARAH VAN SICKLE was born about 1878 in West Virginia.

v.   **MARTHA ANN**[3] **VAN SICKLE** (Anthony[2], Samuel[1]) was born on 15 Oct 1804 in Mason County, Virginia. She died on 02 Feb 1877 in Mason County, West Virginia. She married William Stewart, son of Robert Stewart and Catherine Aleshire on 13 Sep 1823 in Mason County, Virginia. He was born on 09 Sep 1802 in Bath County, Virginia. He died on 16 Jul 1882 in Mason County, West Virginia.

More About Martha Ann Van Sickle:
Burial: Stewart Cemetery, Mason County, West Virginia

Notes for Martha Ann Van Sickle:
Headstone has 1875 for year of death.

More About William Stewart:
Burial: Stewart Cemetery, Mason County, West Virginia
Occupation: 1850 in District 38, Mason County, Virginia; Farmer
Occupation: 1860 in District 1, Mason County, Virginia; Farmer
Occupation: 1870 in Robinson District, Mason County, West Virginia; Farmer
Occupation: 1880 in Robinson District, Mason County, West Virginia; Farmer

William Stewart and Martha Ann Van Sickle had the following children:

    i. JOHN B . [4] STEWART was born on 17 Dec 1824 in Mason County, Virginia. He died on 23 Aug 1900 in Mason County, West Virginia. He married Elizabeth M. (unknown) on 30 Mar 1851 in Jefferson County, Kentucky. She was born on 20 Sep 1827 in Indiana. She died on 05 Sep 1890.

    More About John B. Stewart:
Burial: Stewart Cemetery, Point Pleasant, West Virginia
Occupation: 1850 in Louisville District 1, Jefferson County, Kentucky; Boatman
Occupation: 1860 in District 1, Mason County, Virginia; Can not read occupation on census form.
Occupation: 1870 in Robinson Township, Mason County, West Virginia; Farmer
Occupation: 1880 in Union District, Mason County, West virginia; Farmer

    Notes for John B. Stewart:
John married Elizabeth M. Barbour March 30, 1851 in Jefferson County, Kentucky. In the 1850 U.S. census (August 10, 1850) John Stewart, age 26 and born in Virginia, is living three doors away from James and Elizabeth Barbour in Louisville District 1, Jefferson County, Kentucky. James and Elizabeth are listed as born in Indiana, James age 21 and Elizabeth age 22.

Martha has Kentucky as her place of birth on her death certificate. William F. has Kentucky as his place of birth on his marriage license.

Anthony and Henry have their mothers name as Elizabeth Barbaro and born in Indiana.

    ii.   WILLIAM STEWART was born in 1825 in Mason County, Virginia. He died in 1864. He married Nancy Jane Rice on 31 Jul 1845 in Mason County, Virginia. She was born about 1828 in Mason County, West Virginia. She died after 11 Jun 1880.

    More About William Stewart:
Occupation: 1850 in District 38, Mason County, Virginia; Laborer
Occupation: 1860 in District 1, Mason County, Virginia; Can not read occupation on census form.

    iii.   JULIA ANN STEWART was born on 04 Oct 1827 in Point Pleasant, Mason County, Virginia. She died on 26 May 1902 in Old Town, Mason County, West Virginia. She married Peter Fielding Hawkins, son of Alphonso B. Hawkins and Jane Trimble Poage on 21 Jun 1849 in Mason County, Virginia. He was born on 18 Mar 1822 in Point Pleasant, Mason County, Virginia. He died on 31 Jul 1890 in Point Pleasant, Mason County, West Virginia.

    More About Julia Ann Stewart:
Burial: Lone Oak Cemetery, Point Pleasant, Mason County, West Virginia
Occupation: 1900 in Robinson District, Mason County, West Virginia; Farmer

    iv.   HENRY W. STEWART was born on 16 Dec 1830 in Mason County, Virginia. He died on 30 Aug 1905 in West Columbia, Mason County, West Virginia. He married Deborah McDaniel, daughter of Hutchinson McDaniel and Hannah Johnson on 15 Sep 1862 in Point Pleasant, Mason County, Virginia. She was born on 30 Jul 1843 in Mason County, Virginia. She died on 17 Mar 1900 in Mason County, West

Virginia.

More About Henry W. Stewart:
Burial: 02 Sep 1905 in Stewart Cemetery, Mason County, West
Virginia
Cause Of Death: Brights Disease
Living In: 1860 With his parents in District 1, Mason County, Virginia
Occupation: 1860 in District 1, Mason County, Virginia; Farmer
Occupation: 1870 in Cuivre Township, Pike County, Missouri; Farmer
Occupation: 1880 in Cuivre Township, Pike County, Missouri; Farmer
Occupation: 1900 in Robinson District, Mason County, West Virginia; Farmer

v. CHARLES VOLNEY STEWART was born on 23 Dec 1832 in Mason County, Virginia. He died on 28 Feb 1914 in Mason County, West Virginia. He married Mary Ann White on 27 Dec 1865 in Gallia County, Ohio. She was born on 21 May 1845 in Virginia. She died on 23 Jan 1917 in Mason County, West Virginia.

More About Charles Volney Stewart:
Burial: Stewart Cemetery, Mason County, West Virginia
Living In: 1860 With his parents in District 1, Mason County, Virginia
Living In: 1910 Charles and Mary are living with their son, George, and his family in West Columbia, Mason County, West Virginia.
Occupation: 1870 in West Columbia, Mason County, West Virginia; Grocer
Occupation: 1880 in Clifton, Mason County, West Virginia; Grocer
Occupation: 1900 in West Columbia, Mason County, West Virginia; No Occupation Listed on U.S. Census Form
Occupation: 1910 in West Columbia, Mason County, West Virginia; School Teacher

Notes for Charles Volney Stewart:
Date of death on head stone looks like February 29, 1914 but 1914 was not a Leap Year.

vi. JESSE FRANKLIN STEWART was born on 08 Apr 1835 in Mason County, Virginia. He died on 24 Feb 1910 in Toronto, Jefferson County, Ohio. He married Sarah Catherine Johnson, daughter of David B. Johnson and Jane W. Mulford on 25 Sep 1862 in Meigs County, Ohio. She was born on 23 Jan 1844 in Mason County, Virginia. She died on 18 Jul 1933 in Toronto, Jefferson County, Ohio.

More About Jesse Franklin Stewart:
Burial: Point Pleasant, Mason County, West
Virginia Cause Of Death: Organic Heart Disease
Living In: 1860 With his parents in District 1, Mason County, Virginia
Occupation: 1870 in Robinson Township, Mason County, West Virginia; Farmer
Occupation: 1880 in Robinson District, Mason County, West Virginia; Farmer
Occupation: 1900 in Toronto, Jefferson County, Ohio; Retired Farmer

vii. MARY M. STEWART was born on 26 Oct 1836 in Mason County, Virginia. She died on 17 Jan 1920 in Onawa, Monona County, Iowa. She married James S. Kelly on 30 May 1855. He was born on 26 Jun 1833 in Detroit, Michigan. He died on 06 Oct 1918 in Onawa, Monona County, Iowa.

More About Mary M. Stewart:

Burial: Onawa City Cemetery, Onawa, Monona County, Iowa
Living In: 1860 With her parents in District 1, Mason County, Virginia.
Living In: 1920 Franklin, Monona County, Iowa

8   ELIZABETH STEWART was born on 30 Jan 1839 in Mason County, Virginia. She died on 27 May 1926 in Robinson District, Mason County, West Virginia. She married William McDaniel, son of Hutchinson McDaniel and Hannah Johnson on 19 Dec 1861 in Pleasant Flats, Mason County, Virginia. He was born on 25 Sep 1839 in Mason County, Virginia. He died between 04 Jun 1870 and Jun 1900.

More About Elizabeth Stewart:
Burial: 29 May 1926 in Stewart Cemetery, Mason County, West Virginia
Living In: Dec 1879 Mason County, West Virginia
Living In: 1900 As a widow in Robinson Distict, Mason County, West Virginia.
Living In: 1910 As a widow in Robinson District, Mason County, West Virginia.
Living In: 1920 With her grand daughter, Clara, and her family in Robinson District, Mason County, West Virginia.
Occupation: 1900 in Robinson District, Mason County, West Virginia; Farmer

Notes for Elizabeth Stewart:
Death certificate gives burial place as Stewart Cemetery. Headstone is present in Lone Oak Cemetery.

Elizabeth was present at Madaline's wedding to give permission for Madaline to get married but there is no mention of Madaline's father.
----

9   ZILPHIA R. STEWART was born on 12 Nov 1840 in Mason County, Virginia. She died on 21 Jan 1930 in Point Pleasant, Mason County, West Virginia. She married Cornelius W. White, son of Carlin F. White and Sarah F. Belcher on 05 Nov 1863 in Mason County, West Virginia. He was born on 01 Nov 1840 in Mercer County, Virginia. He died on 02 Nov 1925 in Point Pleasant, Mason County, West Virginia.

More About Zilphia R. Stewart:
Burial: 24 Jan 1930 in Stewart Cemetery, Mason County, West Virginia

x.   JAMES RILEY STEWART was born about 1845 in Mason County, Virginia. He died in May 1875 in Robinson District, Mason County, West Virginia. He married Agnes E. Van Meter, daughter of John VanMeter and Melitha (unknown) on 11 Nov 1868 in Mason County, West Virginia. She was born in Oct 1843 in Mason County, Virginia. She died between 26 Apr 1910-04 Feb 1920.

More About James Riley Stewart:
Occupation: 1970 in Robinson Township, Mason County, West Virginia; Farmer

xi. JOSEPH NEWTON STEWART was born on 29 Nov 1846 in Mason County, Virginia. He died on 22 May 1922 in Point Pleasant, Mason County, West Virginia. He married Margaret Ann Johnson, daughter of David B. Johnson and Jane W. Mulford on 29 Sep 1870 in Mason County, West Virginia. She was born on 20 Feb 1849 in Mason County, Virginia. She died on 28 Aug 1934 in Point Pleasant, Mason County, West Virginia.

More About Joseph Newton Stewart:
Burial: 24 May 1922 in Stewart Cemetery, Mason County, West Virginia
Living In: 1870 With his parents in Robinson District, Mason County, West Virginia.
Occupation: 1870 in Robinson District, Mason County, West Virginia; Farm Worker
Occupation: 1880 in Robinson District, Mason County, West Virginia; Farmer
Occupation: 1900 in Robinson District, Mason County, West Virginia; Farm Laborer
Occupation: 1910 in Robinson District, Mason County, West Virginia; Farmer
Occupation: 1920 in Robinson District, Mason County, West Virginia; Farmer

xii. SARAH J. STEWART was born on 15 Apr 1850 in Mason County, Virginia. She died before 1887. She married Gilbert Van Sickle, son of Samuel Van Sickle and Susan (unknown) on 06 Feb 1868 in Mason County, West Virginia. He was born on 30 Mar 1845 in Mason County, West Virginia. He died on 26 Mar 1930 in Point Pleasant, Mason County, West Virginia.

Notes:

Descendants of Henry Van Meter

Generation 1

2. **HENRY**[1] **VAN METER** . He died in 1803 in Pennsylvania. He married **MARTHA MOORE**. She was born in 1730 in Maryland. She died in 1825 in Pennsylvania.

Henry Van Meter and Martha Moore had the following children:

      i. JESSE[2] VAN METER. She died on 07 Oct 1787 in Pennsylvania.

      ii. JOSEPH VAN METER. He died in 1808.

      iii. MARY VAN METER.

2.   iv. REBECCA VAN METER was born in Green County, Pennsylvania. She died on 28 Dec 1810 in Mason County, Virginia. She married Anthony Van Sickle, son of Samuel Van Sickle and Sarah Thompson on 29 Apr 1789 in Green County, Pennsylvania. He was born about 1770 in New Jersey. He died on 29 Sep 1815 in Mason County, Virginia.

      i.   RACHEL VAN METER was born in 1751 in Pennsylvania.

      ii.   MARTHA VAN METER was born on 24 Dec 1754 in Pennsylvania. She died on 24 Oct 1836 in Pennsylvania.

      iii.   ALICE VAN METER was born on 12 Feb 1756 in Chester, Pennsylvania. She died on 12 Sep 1839 in Ohio.

      iv.   SARAH VAN METER was born on 24 Jun 1758 in Pennsylvania. She died on 12 Sep 1839 in Pennsylvania.

      v.   ELIZABETH VAN METER was born in 1761 in Virginia. She died in 1802.

      vi.   ABSOLOM VAN METER was born in 1765 in Virginia. He died in 1803 in Mason County, Virginia.

      vii.   JOHN VAN METER was born in 1769 in Virginia. He died in 1812 in Mason County, Virginia.

      viii.   PHOEBE VAN METER was born on 08 Jul 1770 in Virginia. She died on 14 Feb 1853.

      ix.   HENRY VAN METER was born in Jun 1773 in Pennsylvania. He died on 13 Dec 1857 in Mason County, Virginia. He married CHRISTINE VAN SICKLE. She was born in Pennsylvania. She died in Mason County, Virginia.

Generation 2

ii.   **REBECCA**[2] **VAN METER** (Henry[1]) was born in Green County, Pennsylvania. She died on 28 Dec 1810 in Mason County, Virginia. She married Anthony Van Sickle, son of Samuel Van Sickle and Sarah Thompson on 29 Apr 1789 in Green County, Pennsylvania. He was born about 1770 in New Jersey. He died on 29 Sep 1815 in Mason County, Virginia.

More About Anthony Van Sickle:
Burial: Point Pleasant, Virginia
Military Service: Mason County, Virginia; Captain of Anthony Van Sickle's Mason County Riflemen in War of 1812.

Anthony Van Sickle and Rebecca Van Meter had the following children:

    i.   HENRY[3] VAN SICKLE was born in 1793 in Green County, Pennsylvania. He died on Nov 1863. He married RACHEL SWAN.

        JESSE VAN SICKLE was born in 1796 in Green County, Pennsylvania.

        HANNAH VAN SICKLE was born in 1798 in Mason County, Virginia.

        ANTHONY VAN SICKLE was born in 1800 in Mason County, Virginia.

iii.   v. ABRAHAM VAN SICKLE was born on 21 Oct 1802 in Mason County, Virginia. He died on 05 Feb 1873. He married MARY RIFFLE. She died after 21 Jun 1870.

iv.   vi. SAMUEL VAN SICKLE was born about 1803 in Virginia.

v.   vii. MARTHA ANN VAN SICKLE was born on 15 Oct 1804 in Mason County, Virginia. She died on 02 Feb 1877 in Mason County, West Virginia. She married William Stewart, son of Robert Stewart and Catherine Aleshire on 13 Sep 1823 in Mason County, Virginia. He was born on 09 Sep 1802 in Bath County, Virginia. He died on 16 Jul 1882 in Mason County, West Virginia.

        JOHN VAN SICKLE was born in 1807 in Mason County, Virginia.

        JOSEPH VAN SICKLE was born on 12 Feb 1809 in Mason County, Virginia. He died on 13 Aug 1884 in Farmington, St. Francois County, Missouri. He married (1) MARY MAHALA HINKLE, daughter of Gideon Hinkle and Rhoda Jane Allen on 26 Dec 1833. She was born about 1815. He married (2) SARAH RICKERT in 1836. She was born on Nov 1816 in Virginia. She died on 16 Dec 1883 in Farmington, St. Francois County, Missouri.

        More About Joseph Van Sickle:
        Burial: 14 Aug 1884 in Farmington, St. Francois County, Missouri
        Occupation: ; Minister

    x. ELI VAN SICKLE was born in 1810 in Mason County, Virginia.

Generation 3

3. **ABRAHAM[3] VAN SICKLE** (Rebecca[2] Van Meter, Henry[1] Van Meter) was born on 21 Oct 1802 in Mason County, Virginia. He died on 05 Feb 1873. He married **MARY RIFFLE**. She died after 21 Jun 1870.

More About Abraham Van Sickle:
Occupation: 1850 in District 38, Mason County, Virginia; Farmer
Occupation: 1860 in District 1, Mason County, Virginia; Farmer
Occupation: 1870 in Robinson Township, Mason County, West Virginia;
Farmer

Abraham Van Sickle and Mary Riffle had the following children:

    i.   ANTHONY[4] VAN SICKLE was born in 1832 in Virginia. He married Magdalen Ann Riffle, daughter of Johnathon Riffle and Nancy (unknown) on 14 Feb 1854 in Marshall County, Virginia. She was born in 1827.

    ii.   GEORGE VAN SICKLE was born in 1835 in Mason County, Virginia. He died on 06

May 1897 in Old Town, Mason County, West virginia. He married LUCY (UNKNOWN).

   iii.   LEWIS J. VAN SICKLE was born on 16 Oct 1838 in Virginia. He died on 30 Dec 1907 in Seymour, Wayne County, Iowa.

More About Lewis J. Van Sickle:
Burial: 30 Dec 1907 in Seymour, Wayne County, Iowa

   iv.   ELI WASHINGTON VAN SICKLE was born on 16 Oct 1838 in Virginia. He died in 1910 in Mason County. WEest virginia. He married Mary Margaret Eckard, daughter of Thomas Eckard and Elizabeth Riffle on 02 Jul 1895 in Point Pleasant, Mason County, West Virginia. She was born on 06 Jun 1847 in Mason County, Virginia. She died on 11 Sep 1928 in Beech Hill, Mason County, West Virginia.

More About Eli Washington Van Sickle:
Burial: Pine Grove Cemetery, Mason County, West Virginia

   v.   CATHERINE VAN SICKLE was born about 1844 in Virginia. She married GEORGE WASHINGTON FOGELSONG.

   vi.   SAMUEL VAN SICKLE was born on 25 Jan 1847 in Mason County, Virginia. He died on 31 Dec 1936 in Beech Hill, Mason County, West Virginia. He married REBECCA JANE BIRCHFIELD. She was born on 05 Oct 1850 in Wyoming County, Virginia. She died on 27 Dec 1936 in Beech Hill, Mason County, West Virginia.

More About Samuel Van Sickle:
Burial: 01 Jan 1937 in Van Sickle Cemetery, Mason County, West Virginia

   vii.   DANIEL C. VAN SICKLE was born about 1850 in Virginia.

4.   **SAMUEL**[3] **VAN SICKLE** (Rebecca[2] Van Meter, Henry[1] Van Meter) was born about 1803 in Virginia.

More About Samuel Van Sickle:
Occupation: 1880 in Robinson District, Mason County, West Virginia; Farmer

Samuel Van Sickle had the following children:

   i.   MARY[4] VAN SICKLE was born about 1855 in Virginia.

   ii.   CATHERINE VAN SICKLE was born about 1874 in West Virginia.

   iii.   STEPHEN VAN SICKLE was born about 1876 in West Virginia.

   iv.   SARAH VAN SICKLE was born about 1878 in West Virginia.

5.   **MARTHA ANN**[3] **VAN SICKLE** (Rebecca[2] Van Meter, Henry[1] Van Meter) was born on 15 Oct 1804 in Mason County, Virginia. She died on 02 Feb 1877 in Mason County, West Virginia. She married William Stewart, son of Robert Stewart and Catherine Aleshire on 13 Sep 1823 in Mason County, Virginia. He was born on 09 Sep 1802 in Bath County, Virginia. He died on 16 Jul 1882 in Mason County, West Virginia.

More About Martha Ann Van Sickle:
Burial: Stewart Cemetery, Mason County, West Virginia

Notes for Martha Ann Van Sickle:
Headstone has 1875 for year of death.

More About William Stewart:
Burial: Stewart Cemetery, Mason County, West Virginia
Occupation: 1850 in District 38, Mason County, Virginia; Farmer
Occupation: 1860 in District 1, Mason County, Virginia; Farmer
Occupation: 1870 in Robinson District, Mason County, West Virginia; Farmer
Occupation: 1880 in Robinson District, Mason County, West Virginia; Farmer

William Stewart and Martha Ann Van Sickle had the following children:

  i. JOHN B . [4] STEWART was born on 17 Dec 1824 in Mason County, Virginia. He died on 23 Aug 1900 in Mason County, West Virginia. He married Elizabeth M. (unknown) on 30 Mar 1851 in Jefferson County, Kentucky. She was born on 20 Sep 1827 in Indiana. She died on 05 Sep 1890.

  More About John B. Stewart:
  Burial: Stewart Cemetery, Point Pleasant, West Virginia
  Occupation: 1850 in Louisville District 1, Jefferson County, Kentucky; Boatman
  Occupation: 1860 in District 1, Mason County, Virginia; Can not read occupation on census form.
  Occupation: 1870 in Robinson Township, Mason County, West Virginia; Farmer
  Occupation: 1880 in Union District, Mason County, West Virginia; Farmer

  Notes for John B. Stewart:
  John married Elizabeth M. Barbour March 30, 1851 in Jefferson County, Kentucky. In the 1850 U.S. census (August 10, 1850) John Stewart, age 26 and born in Virginia, is living three doors away from James and Elizabeth Barbour in Louisville District 1, Jefferson County, Kentucky. James and Elizabeth are listed as born in Indiana, James age 21 and Elizabeth age 22.

  Martha has Kentucky as her place of birth on her death certificate. William F. has Kentucky as his place of birth on his marriage license.

  Anthony and Henry have their mothers name as Elizabeth Barbaro and born in Indiana.

  ii. WILLIAM STEWART was born in 1825 in Mason County, Virginia. He died in 1864. He married Nancy Jane Rice on 31 Jul 1845 in Mason County, Virginia. She was born about 1828 in Mason County, West Virginia. She died after 11 Jun 1880.

  More About William Stewart:
  Occupation: 1850 in District 38, Mason County, Virginia; Laborer
  Occupation: 1860 in District 1, Mason County, Virginia; Can not read occupation on census form.

  iii. JULIA ANN STEWART was born on 04 Oct 1827 in Point Pleasant, Mason County, Virginia. She died on 26 May 1902 in Old Town, Mason County, West Virginia. She married Peter Fielding Hawkins, son of Alphonso B. Hawkins and Jane Trimble Poage on 21 Jun 1849 in Mason County, Virginia. He was born on 18 Mar 1822 in

Point Pleasant, Mason County, Virginia. He died on 31 Jul 1890 in Point Pleasant, Mason County, West Virginia.

More About Julia Ann Stewart:
Burial: Lone Oak Cemetery, Point Pleasant, Mason County, West Virginia
Occupation: 1900 in Robinson District, Mason County, West Virginia; Farmer

iv.　HENRY W. STEWART was born on 16 Dec 1830 in Mason County, Virginia. He died on 30 Aug 1905 in West Columbia, Mason County, West Virginia. He married Deborah McDaniel, daughter of Hutchinson McDaniel and Hannah Johnson on 15 Sep 1862 in Point Pleasant, Mason County, Virginia. She was born on 30 Jul 1843 in Mason County, Virginia. She died on 17 Mar 1900 in Mason County, West Virginia.

More About Henry W. Stewart:
Burial: 02 Sep 1905 in Stewart Cemetery, Mason County, West Virginia
Cause Of Death: Brights Disease
Living In: 1860 With his parents in District 1, Mason County, Virginia
Occupation: 1860 in District 1, Mason County, Virginia; Farmer
Occupation: 1870 in Cuivre Township, Pike County, Missouri; Farmer
Occupation: 1880 in Cuivre Township, Pike County, Missouri; Farmer
Occupation: 1900 in Robinson District, Mason County, West Virginia; Farmer

v.　CHARLES VOLNEY STEWART was born on 23 Dec 1832 in Mason County, Virginia. He died on 28 Feb 1914 in Mason County, West Virginia. He married Mary Ann White on 27 Dec 1865 in Gallia County, Ohio. She was born on 21 May 1845 in Virginia. She died on 23 Jan 1917 in Mason County, West Virginia.

More About Charles Volney Stewart:
Burial: Stewart Cemetery, Mason County, West Virginia
Living In: 1860 With his parents in District 1, Mason County, Virginia
Living In: 1910 Charles and Mary are living with their son, George, and his family in West Columbia, Mason County, West Virginia.
Occupation: 1870 in West Columbia, Mason County, West Virginia; Grocer
Occupation: 1880 in Clifton, Mason County, West Virginia; Grocer
Occupation: 1900 in West Columbia, Mason County, West Virginia; No Occupation Listed on U.S. Census Form
Occupation: 1910 in West Columbia, Mason County, West Virginia; School Teacher

Notes for Charles Volney Stewart:
Date of death on head stone looks like February 29, 1914 but 1914 was not a Leap Year.

----

vi.　JESSE FRANKLIN STEWART was born on 08 Apr 1835 in Mason County, Virginia. He died on 24 Feb 1910 in Toronto, Jefferson County, Ohio. He married Sarah Catherine Johnson, daughter of David B. Johnson and Jane W. Mulford on 25 Sep 1862 in Meigs County, Ohio. She was born on 23 Jan 1844 in Mason County, Virginia. She died on 18 Jul 1933 in Toronto, Jefferson County, Ohio.

More About Jesse Franklin Stewart:
Burial: Point Pleasant, Mason County, West Virginia

Cause Of Death: Organic Heart Disease
Living In: 1860 With his parents in District 1, Mason County, Virginia
Occupation: 1870 in Robinson Township, Mason County, West Virginia;
Farmer
Occupation: 1880 in Robinson District, Mason County, West Virginia; Farmer
Occupation: 1900 in Toronto, Jefferson County, Ohio; Retired Farmer

vii.   MARY M. STEWART was born on 26 Oct 1836 in Mason County, Virginia. She died on 17 Jan 1920 in Onawa, Monona County, Iowa. She married James S. Kelly on 30 May 1855. He was born on 26 Jun 1833 in Detroit, Michigan. He died on 06 Oct 1918 in Onawa, Monona County, Iowa.

More About Mary M. Stewart:
Burial: Onawa City Cemetery, Onawa, Monona County, Iowa
Living In: 1860 With her parents in District 1, Mason County, Virginia.
Living In: 1920 Franklin, Monona County, Iowa

viii.   ELIZABETH STEWART was born on 30 Jan 1839 in Mason County, Virginia. She died on 27 May 1926 in Robinson District, Mason County, West Virginia. She married William McDaniel, son of Hutchinson McDaniel and Hannah Johnson on 19 Dec 1861 in Pleasant Flats, Mason County, Virginia. He was born on 25 Sep 1839 in Mason County, Virginia. He died between 04 Jun 1870-06 Jun 1900.

More About Elizabeth Stewart:
Burial: 29 May 1926 in Stewart Cemetery, Mason County, West Virginia
Living In: Dec 1879 Mason County, West Virginia
Living In: 1900 As a widow in Robinson Distict, Mason County, West Virginia.
Living In: 1910 As a widow in Robinson Distict, Mason County, West Virginia.
Living In: 1920 With her grand daughter, Clara, and her family in Robinson District, Mason County, West Virginia.
Occupation: 1900 in Robinson District, Mason County, West Virginia; Farmer

Notes for Elizabeth Stewart:
Death certificate gives burial place as Stewart Cemetery. Headstone is present in Lone Oak Cemetery.

Elizabeth was present at Madaline's wedding to give permission for Madaline to get married but there is no mention of Madaline's father.

ix.   ZILPHIA R. STEWART was born on 12 Nov 1840 in Mason County, Virginia. She died on 21 Jan 1930 in Point Pleasant, Mason County, West Virginia. She married Cornelius W. White, son of Carlin F. White and Sarah F. Belcher on 05 Nov 1863 in Mason County, West Virginia. He was born on 01 Nov 1840 in Mercer County, Virginia. He died on 02 Nov 1925 in Point Pleasant, Mason County, West Virginia.

More About Zilphia R. Stewart:
Burial: 24 Jan 1930 in Stewart Cemetery, Mason County, West Virginia

x.   JAMES RILEY STEWART was born about 1845 in Mason County, Virginia. He died in May 1875 in Robinson District, Mason County, West Virginia. He married Agnes E. Van Meter, daughter of John VanMeter and Melitha (unknown) on 11 Nov 1868 in Mason County, West Virginia. She was born in Oct 1843 in Mason County,

Virginia. She died between 26 Apr 1910-04 Feb 1920.

More About James Riley Stewart:
Occupation: 1970 in Robinson Township, Mason County, West Virginia; Farmer

xi. JOSEPH NEWTON STEWART was born on 29 Nov 1846 in Mason County, Virginia. He died on 22 May 1922 in Point Pleasant, Mason County, West Virginia. He married Margaret Ann Johnson, daughter of David B. Johnson and Jane W. Mulford on 29 Sep 1870 in Mason County, West Virginia. She was born on 20 Feb 1849 in Mason County, Virginia. She died on 28 Aug 1934 in Point Pleasant, Mason County, West Virginia.

More About Joseph Newton Stewart:
Burial: 24 May 1922 in Stewart Cemetery, Mason County, West Virginia
Living In: 1870 With his parents in Robinson District, Mason County, West Virginia.
Occupation: 1870 in Robinson District, Mason County, West Virginia; Farm Worker
Occupation: 1880 in Robinson District, Mason County, West Virginia; Farmer
Occupation: 1900 in Robinson District, Mason County, West Virginia; Farm Laborer
Occupation: 1910 in Robinson District, Mason County, West Virginia; Farmer
Occupation: 1920 in Robinson District, Mason County, West Virginia; Farmer

xii. SARAH J. STEWART was born on 15 Apr 1850 in Mason County, Virginia. She died before 1887. She married Gilbert Van Sickle, son of Samuel Van Sickle and Susan (unknown) on 06 Feb 1868 in Mason County, West Virginia. He was born on 30 Mar 1845 in Mason County, West Virginia. He died on 26 Mar 1930 in Point Pleasant, Mason County, West Virginia.